Creating a Marriage

James Greteman

PAULIST PRESS
New York/Mahwah, N.J.

Library of Congress Cataloging-in-Publication Data

Greteman, Jim.
    Creating a marriage/James Greteman.
      p. cm.
    Includes bibliographical references.
    ISBN 0-8091-3393-8
    1. Marriage. 2. Communication in marriage. 3. Marriage—
Religious aspects. I. Title.
    HQ734.G748   1993
    646.7'8—dc20   92-42927
                                            CIP

Published by Paulist Press
997 Macarthur Boulevard
Mahwah, New Jersey 07430

Printed and bound in the United States of America

Contents

გურ

Contents

Dedicated to

My family in Iowa
My religious community at Notre Dame
and my many friends

Also to

Victoria Kuhl for editing
and Marilyn Ahlstrom for typing

Preface

§➤

There was once a busy street corner where people rushed by, paying no attention to each other. They were a miscellaneous group, with no connection to each other. Suddenly, a small Volkswagen flew around the corner, and crashed into the front wheel of a very large eighteen-wheeler truck. Now the group of people became a crowd, because there was a center of interest. When the huge truck-driver bounced out of the cab, ripped open the front door of the Volkswagen, pulled out the old grandmother and slapped her, the crowd became a mob.

So, what is marriage? Is it at times like a miscellaneous group of two who pay little attention to each other, or is it sometimes like a crowd with a center of interest, or even a mob?

Marriage is a process, like going up a series of steps with your partner from one floor to another. Like most processes, you take one step at a time. But in marriage, you may want to run or skip certain steps, while your partner may want to stand on one step too long. There are times to get used to each other, times that are exciting, times that are boring, times that are hurting, times that are humorous, times that are happy, and many times when things are just O.K. You will find that your story will be similar to some of the processes and patterns I have described in this book.

1

Parallel with the process of marriage that I will discuss in this book is an overlay of what I call the process of life. That is, in stages of your life, you go through different experiences, and the changes resulting from these experiences affect your relationship with the person you marry. Most of the information I use to describe the process will be based upon Jungian analysis. Carl Jung, a psychiatrist from Zurich, Switzerland, worked with Sigmund Freud but, unlike Freud, he integrated the concept of God into psychotherapy.

This book is based mostly upon my experiences as a clinical marriage and family therapist. After earning my Master's degree, I spent over 5,000 clinical hours in training and workshops with related professionals (psychologists, family therapists, psychiatrists, and clinical social workers). I have had experience in running 600 groups for people whose relationships had failed and who were trying to figure out why, and have also spent the past thirty years sitting with couples and families, listening to what went *right* in their relationships. I have also given many regional and national workshops on failed relationships, marriage, feelings, sexuality, and various other topics. I will draw upon these workshops, my discussions with other people, and my readings, and will share with you what I think helps build successful marriages.

So this book is about what works, and I hope you enjoy comparing your story with the stories in this book. Like I said, marriage is a process of going from one step to another—it's never completed. Neither is your story. One of the key rules that I will emphasize throughout the book is that you go through the steps very gently.

Process of Life

I would like to use an analogy of a stream to illustrate what I call the process of life. It is my belief that each of us is tossed into a stream when we are born, and that we float along this stream of life until we go back to God, or "our Higher Power." While we are in this stream, there are times when it is very calm, and we float along as if we were in a pond, and everything seems to be OK. There are other times when we hit rapids, and it gets exciting or even frightening. At various times we may even try to hold onto a branch along the shore and not continue our journey. But all of us, at one time or another, have to let go of the branch.

In this stream of life, we have a partner who is also in our stream, and we are both floating along together. I believe marriage is the trust or relationship or connection that we have in relationship with each other as we float along. Difficulties may arise when one gets too far ahead or behind, or if one is frightened, or if one doesn't want to move along and stays in one position. I will develop these points further in another section.

I think of this stream of life as having three different parts. The first is the first part of life, in which each of us, as separate people, need to develop the abilities that we need to use in life (mostly in our physical world). This would include our schooling, our early experiences, and the time we start thinking about choosing partners, and whether we want a marriage or we want to be separate. We decide whether or not we want to have a home, and what kind of business or profession we would like to go into. One of our concerns during this time is the sex drive and how we choose to live with that. This is another topic which I will discuss further in another section of the book. During this time, we are going to have to make some decisions, not only about our business or profession, but also about leaving home, choosing a partner, and setting up a relationship.

The second part of the stream is midlife. Midlife is like going out in a sailboat without having much experience of sailing. As we get farther away from the shore, we notice the fog comes in and clouds out one shoreline. So we say, "Well, I'll head for the other shore." Meanwhile, the fog blocks the other shoreline, and we are out in the middle and don't know where we are going. During this time, we tend to be somewhat dissatisfied with ourselves, and with some of the choices we've made. At midlife we need to get more in touch with our feelings and our choices. Just because we are dissatisfied with one thing or another doesn't mean we have to throw out everything. So this is a time to be very careful, to go very slowly down the stream.

The third part of the stream is the latter part of life. Just as the first part of life has to do with the outer world, this part has to do with the inner world—examining certain paths that we have used to come down the stream, and whether or not we want to continue in that direction, checking out our values, and whether or not we want to keep them or adopt some new ones. Changes going on in our unconscious minds require more quiet time, and a sense of power develops that many religions associate with rebirth or renewal.

In Love

§❧

So here you are, floating down the stream of life, probably a fairly young person, or at least young mentally and spiritually. As you float along, you have a new experience; you notice somebody else floating in the stream of life rather close to you. Virginia Clemente, a marriage and family therapist, says that this is when Psychology 101 begins. This is the time when you use all of your ability to get across that stream and meet that other person, because for some reason that person is very special to you. I would call this "falling in love." Now there are a number of problems with falling in love. The first one is that we only do this, whether consciously or unconsciously, when we are sexually motivated (erotic experience).

The second problem is that falling in love is a temporary experience. It doesn't mean that you later cease loving the person, but that particular "in love" feeling, like all feelings, tends to pass, just as any honeymoon will pass. Let me give you an example of what I am talking about. When I was a baby, about one or two months old, I basically had no boundaries. I experienced myself—when I waved my arms and my legs I was the world and the world was me. I didn't make a distinction between myself, the crib, or the room. But at a later stage, I started to realize, probably when I hit myself in the head a few times, that my arm was connected to me. Or, when I started following people with my eyes, I realized that there was somebody else out there. Or if I was hungry, and Mom and Dad didn't always come because I had been yelling three or four times an hour, they may have left me sit a little bit. So I was starting to find out there is something "out there." In other words, I started to establish boundaries.

At about the age of two these boundaries are tested, and that is what they call the "terrible twos." The child becomes the little King or Queen of the Mountain. He/she thinks, "Everybody else is supposed to wait on me, including the dog!" But others start helping the child realize that certain things are not going to happen.

As we age, we continue to build boundaries around ourselves and as we are floating in the stream of life, these boundaries can become pretty well-defined. We may then start having a problem with loneliness. This is a pretty normal experience, especially for teenagers, who experience a lot of problems with loneliness. So a teenager will tend to fall in love to resolve this problem. Because falling in love means there are no boundaries, the person tries to solve the problem by merging with another.

So you see this person in the stream, you fall in love and everything is wonderful! But, as I said, the honeymoon always ends, because anybody can fall in love. It doesn't take any effort. It is simply a feeling. What tends to happen is that eventually the two people start talking about money or a place to live, a bank account, a car. One person may say, "Let's go out and eat tonight." The other might say, "No, I think we should save our money so we can buy this." Eventually, the boundaries start building back up, and pretty soon one or both individuals start saying, "I am not sure I love this person." So, falling in love is simply a feeling, and feelings tend to pass.

Now what is real love? M. Scott Peck, in his book *The Road Less Traveled*, defines love this way: "The will to extend one's self for the purpose of nurturing one's own or another's spiritual growth." So, in essence, I would say real love is a circular process, combining love for the other and self-love, that is, loving yourself with the love for another. Now, to do this, one needs to extend one's own boundaries. This is called growth.

To experience growth, one needs to reach out, and in this process there is first an attraction, and that other person seems to be very special in some way. It becomes an investment because we are putting something into it. We hope that that person, if it is real love, will do the same. Last of all, there is a commitment. Both people are putting some energy into it. Through this, we are enlarging ourselves, stretching our boundaries. And we are growing.

Growth tends to take place with what is familiar. That is, what is familiar to us in the other person tends to resonate with us. Each time we try to define real love, we are toying with the idea of a mystery. Some call it Eros, Philie, Agape, or perfect love as opposed to imperfect love. If we want to develop what I call real love with a partner in the stream of life, the first thing we have to do is shift away from our individualistic thrust, doing our own thing, and commit ourselves to the relationship.

Often we will have to distance ourselves from our previous families or at least from parents, so that we can start making decisions along with this new person. If we stay too enmeshed with the previous parental system, we could have difficulty, because the other person won't fit into the system.

And last of all in developing this real love, one must strengthen what I would call one's collective identity with this other person. The problem is that both of us are humans and we tend to make mistakes. So there is going to be a negative part of this relationship that is developing along with real love.

So, what makes this other person special to us? Probably telling and showing their love to us. How important is this other person to you? There is a special feeling for this other person, and they really count with us. Another difficulty can develop because the couple expects happiness; in other words, we have very high expectations of each other. We expect to receive love, develop a friendship with each other, have a satisfying sex life, and a close time of sharing parenting. Most people expect to be happy—it's the dream state that we imagine for marriage.

But to develop these things, we have to spend some time, and unless we spend that time, and unless we work on these particular things, nothing is going to happen. Most couples go through what is called the mating instinct time, and then they may cool off, and want to leave each other at that stage. But this is the opportunity for genuine love. Because genuine, or real love, is a decision, a commitment. It takes time—we have to work at it, which means we have to listen to each other. It takes courage, which means that we have to risk something.

Loving is always risking. We risk on different levels, when we love a plant, a pet, or a partner. M. Scott Peck says, "The only real security in life lies in relishing life's insecurities." Along with attention and risk and time, we have to make a commitment. We have to put in some discipline. Discipline, to most people, is a negative word. But in this case, discipline means delaying some gratification, accepting some responsibility for one's self, telling the truth and being dedicated to reality. Finally, we must put some balance into the relationship.

Real love is the essence, then, of a true marriage. A psychiatrist, H. B. Dicks, observed that the marriage is the "nearest adult equivalent to the original child-parent relationship." Real love has to be worked at, and it helps to expand one's boundaries and stretch one's self. Sexual orgasm can also mean expanding one's boundary, a feeling of ecstasy, the losing touch with time and space, being outside of oneself—becoming one with the universe. This may only happen for several seconds, but this oneness is actually like the mystical union with the higher power.

So, in summary, I would say that falling in love is a feeling, not the reality. Real love is the basis for forming a marriage, and this takes time. Falling in love has a grain of truth in it, so it can actually be a foretaste of what is to come. I believe most couples fall in love through their feelings, and then work their way into what I would call real love. Real love has three conditions, according to John Powell: 1) I am on your side; 2) I know you have good qualities; 3) I am going to help you develop them. By extending and stretching boundaries, we now have one of the main ingredients for putting together a marriage—a commitment to each other, not a feeling. So, in the stream of life we take on a partner, and we hold hands as we go down the stream. At first there are going to be some difficulties, but we are nevertheless willing to take the risk to do that which is called marriage.

The Marriage Ceremony

৯৯

When we have fallen in love and have made a decision to get married, the first thing that we plan is some type of ceremony for the occasion. In planning this ceremony, we are floating down that stream and holding hands with our partner, and we want something special—we want family and friends, who support us in the style of life we have planned, to be present at our ceremony. So, over a period of time, we choose the invitations, the favors, the colors, and the dresses, or whatever special things we need. Will we have a dinner or a dance, or just a small reception? We wonder what the church or chapel is going to look like. The colors of the candles, the flowers, and everything —all of this planning adds to the excitement and anticipation.

I recently went to a wedding, and noticed that the usher took each person to the side of the aisle that had the family system that each person belonged to. There was quite a large crowd, and we were all happy, filled with expectation, as we looked at each other across the aisle. There was so much bliss in the group. Everybody was wearing their finest clothes, because it was a very special occasion. There was music playing, and the atmosphere was just right. We knew that the ceremony was going to start when they unrolled a carpet down the center aisle. Just as the ceremony was beginning, the men came out and stood up in front with the groom, along with the other people who represented the groom's side of the family.

Three little boys came in with three little girls—they were all about the age of three or four. The little boys were wearing black pants and white shirts, with red suspenders and red bow ties. The little girls were all decked out in white dresses with red sashes, with red bows in their hair. Each of these six small children carried a basket of flower petals, and they sprinkled them down the aisle as they walked. As they came down the aisle, they threw the flower petals here and there (I don't suppose they practiced this earlier, since you wouldn't want to give three and four year olds baskets of flowers the night before). Everyone was smiling because they looked so cute. Halfway down the aisle, they got all bunched up at one point, and one little girl threw a handful of flower petals at one of the little boys. The six of them began having a flower fight! Everyone stood on the pews, taking pictures and laughing, and the six little ones had their flower fight until they got rid of all the flower petals.

So the planned ceremony went on, and the beautiful young girls and the bride came down the aisle. In this case, it was a religious ceremony, and it was very beautiful. There were tears shed on the right and the left sides of the aisle, which often happens when these rituals take place. The young couple made their promises—they had written their own vows, which were beautifully expressed. They spoke of supporting each other in better times and in worse, and they used different analogies to express their vows.

With a little laughter, everyone loosened up, and the couple, as well as the two families, seem to become more like one. Then the couple went off to the honeymoon. I always laugh when I sit with couples here in my office, because when I see them riding off on their honeymoon, the two are as one, as if there were only one person in the car. Again the rituals—the streamers and the writing on the car, the cans or balloons—contribute to the excitement and high anticipation. But a week later, after the honeymoon, they come back, and one is looking out of the right window and one is looking out of the left window. It is as if they are two people once again.

It is exciting to plan a wedding ceremony, but it is hard to plan a marriage. When we get married, we make certain promises and we have very high expectations. Whenever we have high expectations, there is a tendency for things to get worse for us before they get better. Marriage is a process, and the worst part is that we promise totally unconditional love. But, like the process of falling in love, there is a down side to it. I am not sure that we can have unconditional love, at least not at first. I believe that we can have conditional love at first, and if we are willing to work at it, we will end up having unconditional love for each other. Marriage is like a crucible—for better or for worse—and we will have to go through some painful changes. I am not trying to scare you—I am simply saying that we must be realistic about what marriage is. Marriage doesn't make us happy. It doesn't provide for our individual growth, or solve the different personal problems that we need to work on. A marriage is simply a style of living.

We are going to discuss five stages of marriage, and then we will talk about some different styles of marriage. Again, it is a process, and like any process, there is a beginning, middle, and end.

As we go down the stream of life on our trip back to God, we will probably be holding hands with somebody. In other words, we choose a particular partner on the journey back to God.

Marriage

ও৯

There are many ways of looking at marriage. I find Susan Campbell's ideas, from her book *The Couple's Journey,* to be enlightening and useful, so I am going to use her five stages. In my discussion of each stage, I will introduce you to a couple. Keep in mind that these stages do overlap—and if one person is farther ahead than the other, this may cause some difficulties.

The first stage is the romantic stage. This is the honeymoon period, when a young couple first gets married. In our case, we'll talk about Mark and Tricia White, a young couple who are still in the process of leaving home, and who have been married for two months. Mark is twenty years old and unemployed, and Tricia is eighteen years old and works at Burger King. At this early stage in their marriage, both Mark and Tricia are high on the promise, the shared dream, the vision of what they want to have. Both deny that there are any differences in their feelings. They are floating along the stream of life, holding hands and paying very little attention to anyone else around them. At this time, Mark and Tricia have not looked at any joint problem-solving techniques, and they are basically counting on hope for answers to any problems. Everything is rosy—the intimacy is very intense, and they only see what they want to see. Their perceptions are like tunnel vision—they only see each other, and potential problems are glossed over. They are not disclosing very much about themselves yet, so everything goes on wonderfully.

This is basically a feeling stage, and one of the tasks of this stage is for the couple to start to disclose information about themselves—but not all at once, because it is best not to over-whelm our partner too soon. This stage is usually a lot of fun, but it is basically an illusion. At the end of this stage, there start to be a few cracks in the system. Suddenly we will notice how our partner leaves a wet towel by the tub, or dirty socks on the floor, or how our partner leaves the dirty dishes in the sink and never cleans them up.

The second stage is called the power stage. Our couple this time is Randy and Becky Green. The two of them have been married three years. Randy is a graduate student, and Becky works in a bank. Becky is seven months pregnant. Randy is 24 years old and Becky is 26. During the power stage, each individual starts telling his or her story, and the differences between the two people become very pronounced. Randy says, "But you aren't the person who I thought I married!" Becky spends all of her time trying to make Randy into what she wants. Both partners at this stage experience hurt feelings, and are pulling away from each other. Disillusionment is setting into the marriage. This is one of the most dangerous times in a marriage; sometimes we will want to go back home and just forget the whole thing. There may be many angry feelings and each will express his or her needs in a different way. For example, Randy might ignore Becky, or he might try to coax her to do what he wants her to do. If he loses control, he may end up threatening her. Becky may use her wiles, and she may cry if she doesn't get her way. She might act helpless or try to seduce him. In the end, she gets angry, and withdraws. Randy also gets angry and withdraws.

The conflict at this stage is based upon the child part of the personality. As I mentioned earlier, this is the part of us which basically just wants to be taken care of. But then, at some stage, we want our independence. We set up boundaries, and when we got married we decided to let someone else inside of our boundaries. But we are not too sure about the trustworthiness of those whom we let inside. Rather than learning to stretch our boundaries, we sometimes use the techniques we learned in our family systems. If our family used shouting to solve problems, then we might use shouting. If our family used withdrawal, and never talked about problems—just letting the pain linger on— then we might use that. So each of us needs to ask ourselves, "What pattern did I pick up from my family?"

Another aspect of the conflict between Randy and Becky is that men and women tend to look at things differently. Randy, like most men, tends to be goal-centered and into problem solving. As a result of this orientation, he may seem to be insensitive. Becky might be more relationship centered, and would want to have a heart-to-heart discussion about feelings, not necessarily with the aim of solving a particular problem. I will discuss these tendencies later in the book.

In the power stage, both partners get into what is called "payback time," or "spite time." This can go on for quite some time, and can introduce much coldness into a relationship. Sometimes we'll wonder who we married and why we married this person. To work through this stage, Randy and Becky need to accept equal responsibility for whatever the problem is. They need to get past the blaming attitude of, "Well, you know how men are . . . how women are." In other words, putting each other in categories and boxes isn't helpful. Boxes are fine for storing clothes, but they don't work very well for partners. Once we realize that both of us are equally responsible for the state of our relationship, we are ready to make a choice as to what we want to do to resolve our differences.

The third stage is called the stability stage. The couple we'll use for an example here are Jerry and Ellen Grey. They have been married for twenty years. Jerry is 44 years old, and he is a farmer; 42-year-old Ellen is a nurse. Ellen had a miscarriage early in the marriage, and isn't able to have any more children. They eventually agreed to adopt three children.

For Ellen and Jerry, the stability stage started when they began to forgive each other. In other words, they both recognized that Jerry had faults just like Ellen had faults. Both agreed to let go of the effort to change each other. For instance, Ellen let go of the idea that she was going to change Jerry into a more perfect partner. They both began to focus more on the outside world. Both partners use problems to learn more about themselves rather than to get into blaming and using the other as a scapegoat.

Jerry had learned about conflict, and about the times that he needed to pull back in the relationship, just as Ellen had learned that Jerry had vulnerabilities in certain areas. Both of them started to see how much their growing confidence in themselves and in their relationship allowed them to give the other the space he or she needed. The problem-solving techniques which they developed at this time were not just Jerry's or Ellen's, but belonged to both of them. They looked at both of their family systems and decided what kind of behavior they wanted to use in their system, and what they wanted to stop using.

Both Jerry and Ellen began to be more gentle with themselves, as well as with each other. During this stage, the two partners can be thought of as guiding each other through the stream of life, rather than trying to force each other to go in a given direction. As a result of these understandings, their marriage became more neutral, especially in the area of problem solving. The difficulty and the challenge that the couple experiences at this stage is that they could get too comfortable, and may not want to continue growing. Growth demands a certain amount of risk and uncertainty.

The fourth stage is the commitment stage, and we'll talk about Jack and Bev Black. Jack is 56 years old, and he is a construction foreman. Bev is 54 and a part-time teacher. They have been married for 33 years, and have four children. Since Jack and Bev gave up trying to remodel each other, they both have been able to take responsibility for what works in their relationship. Both can be assertive when they need to be, when discussing what needs to be done around the home. Both can be assertive about play, also. Jack and Bev don't seem to be very rigid at this time. When they fight, they both accept what needs to be changed and get involved—they are both committed to the relationship. They have learned that each partner has a nice side and a dark side, and they've learned to live with their mistakes.

They may still have doubts and fears about the relationship at times, but they know they can pull it off. Each has learned to live with life's uncertainties and ups-and-downs. It is as if they are sitting on a teeter-totter—they have learned to create a balance in their relationship. One thing that Jack and Bev like about this stage is that there is more separateness, but it is comfortable and they remain aware of where they are in the relationship. They have created a marriage system that works with the paradoxes of life. As one couple told me, they know that their partner will save the last dance for them.

The last stage, the co-creation stage, is personified by another couple, Hank and Eva Gold. Hank is 76 years old, a retired business person. Eva is 74, and has worked in the home. They had six children, with five still living. One died in early infancy. Hank and Eva have been married for 57 years.

Hank and Eva have learned that love is something they can prepare for, but can't control. The word "control," in fact, doesn't enter into their lives much at this time. They've learned to look past parenting for the meaning in their lives, since the kids are now adults. They have learned to look past jobs, because they have done what they wanted to do. They have even looked past sex, although they still enjoy each other immensely. They experience no contradiction between what we might call self-love and love for the partner. They are past the idea of "what's in it for me," and they know that the relationship is solid.

Their relationship is, for them, less a dependence than an interdependence. They have learned to bring the pieces together, as if they had assembled a large jigsaw puzzle, knowing they could put all the pieces together, yet still with more pieces to find and fit into the puzzle. After these many years, they are still growing in intimacy.

There is a story I would like to tell about this couple. I was curious about whether they ever fight. When I asked them about this, Eva looked at Hank and laughed, saying that they "really had some good ones." He smiled at her with a special twinkle in his eyes. She returned the smile, like they knew something I did not know. Hank then said that they still fight once in a while, but not for very long. It takes energy to stay mad. I asked them how they worked it out. Hank said that when they got married, they made an agreement on their honeymoon that every week they would go out together for a half-hour for coffee. For 57 years they have been doing this. Eva said that it is difficult to sit across from a person you're really mad at, for a half-hour, and stay mad. By putting aside this time to spend together, they made sure that there was time and energy to work on the relationship.

In conclusion—as we float down the stream of life, and take the path of marriage, we will experience different stages. These stages are not distinct, and will overlap. As we think about the descriptions of these stages, we'll find some things that fit and others that don't. Our own particular situation is unique, but thinking about the tasks of these stages can help us in dealing with our own situation.

It can be fun to float down the stream of life, holding hands with somebody. Other times it will be exciting, dull, very interesting, or just average—depending on what is going on in our lives at the time, and at what stage we are in in our marriage.

Intimacy

$\wp$

Intimacy means a readiness to risk ourselves in a relationship with someone else—in the case of marriage, with our spouse. It has been said many times that we are born alone and die alone. But as we float through the stream of life, it is comforting to know that there are others nearby, floating through the stream with us. In the case of marriage, there is someone very special travelling with us.

I believe that intimacy requires three elements. The first one is exclusiveness. The five couples that I spoke about earlier had set up an exclusive relationship between themselves and their partners. This is one of the factors which helps keep the relationship strong. The second factor is having not only a feeling of love, but a commitment. Commitment is very important in making marriage work. Last of all, these couples were willing to share their many successes and failures in life. So exclusiveness, commitment, and sharing are the elements that are necessary for intimacy. But not everyone who is married always has these three elements, and this is where many problems can begin.

Many times one of the partners will attempt to control the other in terms of potential intimacy, and the other partner may totally withdraw. When this happens, a situation of isolation exists. Isolation can sabotage a marriage. We often use this isolation as a shield against looking at some of our own issues, things that are going on in our own lives that we'd rather not deal with.

Let me give you an example. One of the conditions involved in creating a good life is to get to know ourselves and what is going on in our own personalities, learning to accept the different parts of ourselves. This is a great paradox, in the sense that whenever we have self-awareness we have a certain amount of anxiety. In a marriage, people sometimes try to eradicate this anxiety by clinging to each other. Clinging in a relationship is not intimacy; it is an example of fusion. The difficulty with fusion is that you may have physical closeness, but the boundaries between the two individuals are dissolved, and it is important for a person to maintain a certain degree of separateness.

I'd like to develop this concept of isolation further. The first type of isolation I see as a space between the person and him/herself. This is usually called intrapersonal isolation. Parts of ourselves which we don't want to accept or deal with are closed off because they are too painful or unpleasant to deal with. The second type of isolation is with another person. If we lack social skills and the personality style needed to make an intimate social interaction, we will choose to isolate ourselves rather than be exposed to our own inadequacies in the interpersonal area.

The third type of isolation is what is called existential loneliness. This is related to the physical gap between ourselves and others. As I sit here in my office with a couple, there is a space between them, between me and the wife, and between me and the husband. This existential isolation can never be resolved in a marriage, because it cannot be resolved until we go back to God. So if we tried to resolve that in a marriage, it would create an unreal expectation.

So there are different forms of isolation to deal with as we float together down the stream of life. By taking time to realize where we are with these issues, we can learn to create more of a balance that moves us toward intimacy. We can start developing what I call the virtue of love.

Loneliness is another aspect of the intimacy issue. Many times I come into my office and sit down, close the door, and look out the window. I may see children playing across the street, or people walking their dogs, but I am alone. I have a choice—I can get up, go outside, and engage with other people, or I can remain alone. If I want to be close to others, I have to go out and talk to them, taking the risk of rejection over and over again. So loneliness can develop from the fear of that rejection. If I don't reach out, I can be with other people and still be extremely lonely. Another kind of loneliness is existential loneliness—again, the space between us, the space that can only be filled when we go back to God. So in this respect loneliness is a normal part of life; if this is bothering you, it helps to check with yourself to see what is going on. A marriage can help us with the first, but not the second kind of loneliness.

Children

ॐ

Children are most like us in their feelings and least like
us in their thinking.

David Elkind
Children and Adolescents

In this chapter, I will discuss parenting and children. I
would like to tell you three stories. The first story is about a
young couple who were moving to a new home. They were
called by the realtor, who said that they had to be out of their
old home by a certain time, because a couple was coming to see
their house. The mother, who had small children, was late getting out of the house, and she met the couple at the front door.
The little three year old looked at the couple and asked, "Are
you coming to look at our house?" They said "Yes," and
smiled. Now this little three year old had always been very nice
and polite. But now she looked at them and said, "Well, I have a
whole bunch of dolls upstairs and I don't want anybody touching them, because I don't want fingerprints on them." The
mother, as she told me later, nearly died of embarrassment,
because this was not like her little daughter. The point I am
trying to make is that we should enjoy our children—they are
only children once in our lifetimes.

23

The second story is this. A mother and father were having a disagreement on a Saturday. The father was going down to the office to work, and the mother told him that she wanted him home by 5:00 that afternoon, so that they could go to church. Apparently, there was some difficulty early in the morning and at noon over this matter. The children were watching this disagreement unfold. As time went by, the mother got more and more upset, and showed some of her hurt feelings. At 5:00, the father didn't show up, so the mother packed up the children and went off to church. As they sat in church, ten minutes went by, and it was pretty crowded by this time. The father came into the church and pushed into the pew next to his family. The mother gave him a wilting look, and the father hung his head a little because he knew that he was supposed to have been home, and he hadn't been there. Meanwhile, one of their children, a little four year old, was watching, and said, "Daddy, Mommy is really angry at you." About 150 people behind him in the pews exploded in laughter as they watched the whole affair. Children pick up on our actions very clearly, and they sometimes can embarrass us, but as I say, enjoy them, because they are still our children.

The third story is about a little two and a half year old, just starting to speak. He didn't really know the meaning of words yet. He was playing with some of the children next door, who had a new puppy. There was concern about the puppy, because the puppy had just spent the day at the veterinarian's office. The little boy came in while we were all sitting there, and explained to us that the puppy next door had to go to the hospital to be "shoveled." We did not quite know what getting a dog "shoveled" was all about, but we finally figured out that the little dog next door was spayed. The young one didn't quite know the meaning of words yet, so both shoveled and spayed were in the same category.

We adults need to enjoy our children for what they are—

namely, children. They will show us patterns that we ourselves have shown them.

The Blacks used a practice with their children that is a good example of a pattern that parents could use. They were especially concerned about listening to their children. When the children would complain or cry, or when they were happy about something, the Blacks made a point of listening carefully to the children's feelings, letting the children share their feelings with them. Because they have experienced this careful listening, the Blacks believe, their children, when they grow up, will have the ability to share their feelings with other adults, and especially with their partner in marriage.

Jerry and Ellen Gray always talked about acceptance with their children. They accepted each child as he/she was, and they did not make comparisons between their children.

The Golds put emphasis on kindness with their children. They believed that if they showed lots of kindness, compassion, and patience with their children, that when they grew to be adults, they would pass that pattern on to their children. Kindness is important during the times when it is particularly difficult to be close to the child; such as when the child is trying to sort out his/her separateness, and move away from the family.

With these qualities of kindness, patience, and compassion, parents can be very firm with their children. They can expect certain things from them, they can hold up certain value systems to the children, saying, "this is what we expect of you." When their children don't live up to the expectations, the parents can state rather firmly that they expect the child to live up to the particular standard that the family has. The child should feel free to discuss this with the parents, but in the end the parents will still want that particular pattern or value in their family system. When the qualities of kindness, patience, and compassion underlie our efforts to instill values, we stand a much greater chance of our children's acceptance of our values.

As parents, we all struggle with how to best raise our children. We can succeed if we follow some basic, flexible patterns, like sitting down and discussing things with our children on their level. The couples that we spoke about based their ideas on parenting around acceptance, kindness, openness to the truth, listening, patience, compassion, firmness, and respect for the uniqueness of each child. We still have a right to state what we expect of our children, and when our parenting is based on these principles, our children will respond positively to our expectations.

I will always remember the statement of Eva Gold. She said that unless we listen to the children's feelings—and they will share their feelings when they are small—how will they learn to share feelings later on in life, when they are married? I believe that this is one of the most important things that parents have to learn in regard to their children. We must take the time to listen to our children, especially on the feeling level.

As parents, we need to affirm to ourselves that we are doing a pretty good job of raising our children. We can't expect to be perfect, but we need to compliment ourselves on the good job we are doing. Sometimes we need to look at our patterns of childrearing and ask ourselves: "What options do we have in this particular situation?" or, "What should we do with this adolescent who is out of line?" We need to talk these things over with our partner.

There are several other key patterns that are particularly useful to keep in mind. The first is that we should never do for children what they can do for themselves. Another one is to make special time for each child, to go out of our way to do something special with each child, whether it's going to the store, or simply playing catch in the backyard. One book that I recommend to all parents who come into my office is Frank Main's *Perfect Parenting and Other Myths*. I believe this book can help those of us who doubt our abilities to parent properly in certain situations.

Like marriage, good parenting is a process, something learned over time and we should allow ourselves that time. We can learn some of the skills from books, and from talking with other parents about situations that they experienced with their children. All parents should hug their children a lot. It is especially important for fathers to hug their sons and daughters. I have seen many men in my office over the years and it is amazing to me how many of them can tell me the exact moment that their fathers let them sit on their lap for the last time. This shows how meaningful affection is, and how important it is for fathers—as well as mothers, who naturally seem to do this more—to show affection to their sons and daughters. If we do this, when our children become adults, they will be more affectionate, and will be willing to show this affection to their partners. If we go slow on parenting, and keep telling ourselves that we are doing a reasonably good job, we are doing all that we are expected to do as a parent.

I have one final caution for all parents of small children. It is important to regulate the amount of time children spend watching television, especially the sitcoms. Many of these comedies use negative put-downs in their portrayals of family life. When children see this, they tend to pick up these patterns. In contrast, if we learn to use positive approaches with each other in our marriage, and then with our children, then our children will imitate these positive patterns, and will treat us and each other in the same positive way.

Gender

ç∂

The gender roles which we have in our marriages—that is, we have a male in one boat and a female in the other as we go down the stream of life—have led to many misunderstandings. Most of us were brought up in families that had certain patterns of behavior for males and others for females. For example, males tend to dominate certain discussions, and women often lack confidence and hesitate to communicate their ideas. In certain family systems, women habitually defer to men. That is, the men are fed first, or the men interrupt more often.

Let's look at some of the messages about gender that our five couples may have received from their original families. Did Hank, for instance, learn that "Big boys don't cry," or did Eva learn that girls don't invite boys out? All kinds of messages are given to us by religious organizations, the people in the neighborhood, our friends, and most of all, our families. You will notice some of these if you check yourself out—for example, if you cook out, maybe you'll wear an apron and your partner wears an apron. What are the messages on these aprons? When you drive around town, what are the messages on the bumper stickers? Some of these are rather crude, and some are definitely very male-oriented, while others are very female-oriented. Or the next time you go to the circus, see if you can find a woman ring master. We can see as we read through a magazine, the gender messages that are given to us through cartoons and other illustrations.

In the previous chapter, we talked about what intimacy is and isn't. Our question for this chapter is, does a male consider intimacy from a certain position, and a female from another position? For example, males tend to be more oriented toward the physical, sexual aspects of a relationship, while women tend to be more into the emotional side of the relationship. Some families tend to think of women as emotional butterflies, while men are thought of as much more solid. All of these things that we bring into our marriage from our families affect us and our partner in our journey through life.

An interesting exercise for a couple, no matter where they are in their marriage, is to make a list of some of the messages received from their families as they grew up, especially the messages about sexuality. What were some of the differences between the messages that were given to different members of the family—our brothers versus our sisters? These messages affect how we relate as adults now, and have a big impact on the patterns of our marriages. Many of us receive messages like, "Men don't cry," and so women find it unsettling when men cry. Women are often trained never to approach men, so we may have a pattern of passivity, which won't help when we need to say something.

Which messages work and don't work? Which gender messages do we want to pass on to our children? We can ask each other what the rules and regulations were that our parents taught us. We can also talk about the behaviors of other members of the family.

We might ask: "What did they teach you about being a woman or a girl in the family where you came from?" Or a man or a boy? Or, what did we learn about a particular behavior pattern, like crying? How did our parents treat a male family member when he cried? How did they treat a girl when she cried?

In the family we also learn about relationships. We can ask each other, "What did they teach you about relationships, about what happens when two people get married?" What our partner learned and what we learned might be different. It is good to reflect with your partner what might have happened if we had been born a member of the other sex. How would our lives have been different, and what are the responsibilities that we would have had when we were small? Another exercise is to observe a group, in a class, a playground, a mall, or anywhere, and give each other feedback on what would be male and female behavior of the people going by.

One might ask why we would want to go through some of these exercises. Part of the reason is to understand how male and female interactions influence us as we are in our boats, reaching back and forth toward each other. The ongoing dialogue is influenced by these factors, and knowing about them helps us understand the weaving back and forth. We know more about where our partner is coming from, and about some of our own motivations. Becoming aware of these patterns can make our actions clearer to us, and can help us evaluate them and decide whether we want to continue them or make changes.

Expanding

§☙

In this chapter, I'd like to expand our discussion of the gender aspects of the marriage relationship. When fresh winds blow on our boats as we go through the stream of life, we can sometimes become extremely frightened. As a result of this fear, one partner may start stonewalling, while the other becomes extremely critical. One pulls back, while the other goes on the attack with criticism. If this pattern is followed, it can lead to much difficulty in the relationship. Rather than using these two ways of responding to change, we need to look at ourselves and the ways we react when changes in our partners push us into new territories.

An example would be when a wife who has always been home goes out and starts working. This will change the pattern of the marriage. By making a change, a shadowy, anxiety-ridden landscape is created for the other partner. The husband may complain, "We never get a decent meal around here anymore," and he may feel that he is not being taken care of. This type of situation can become intimidating to the male, who may have learned in his family of origin that he should be the breadwinner.

These types of adjustments take time. One thing we can do to help these transitions is to develop more supportive friendships outside the family. Then when we do come home, we can give a little bit more and be more nurturing. Nurturing isn't just a job for Mom—it's for the husband as well as the wife.

A common pattern I see in my office is that if a wife goes off to work, she still keeps all of her old responsibilities, that is, all of the work in the house. This is unfair and creates resentment. A recent study showed that when men get involved in doing housework—not just being told what to do, but seeing what has to be done and doing it—they live longer. Similarly, when a man becomes a nurturing, involved, committed father, he becomes more emotionally supportive of his wife. As a result, the whole family changes for the better.

Problems in this area go back to how we were parented. If a boy had little support from his father, he may not know how to give or receive support. The poet, Robert Bly, talks about how to maintain the strength and goodness of male identity within the family, which will enhance—not detract from—the ability to be nurturing, caring, and involved. One of the things to do is to reach out to other males, to form a supportive group, where we can learn to see other men not just as softball partners or golf buddies or whatever, but as close friends with whom we can be intimate and vulnerable.

As Dad learns how to cook and do things around the house while Mom goes off to work, it's important for Mom to sit back and let him make his mistakes and do it his way. These household jobs should become "our" jobs, things that we take turns at doing.

In the last chapter, we spoke of the two genders, male and female. But actually, when we start out in life, we are identical. Young boys learn how to be men by watching their fathers, just as females learn to be women by watching their mothers or other special women. I have a very strong belief that men can learn to temper their masculinity, which is often exaggerated by learning, especially well by helping to take care of children.

Each of us, male and female, must stop blaming the other and take responsibility for ourselves and for the relationship. We start taking responsibility by doing our share. A sociologist, Arlie Hochschild, stated, "The happiest two job marriages I saw during my research were the ones in which the men and women shared the housework and parenting . . . making it to the school play, helping a child to read, cooking dinner in good spirits, remembering the grocery list, taking responsibility for cleaning up the bedroom—these were the silver and gold of the marital exchange."

Taking housework seriously means seeing what needs to be done, thinking about it, planning, and doing some of the work. It is not the same as having our partner assign chores for us to do. Taking this responsibility means that men can have their virtues, like courage, persistence, generosity, loyalty, and self-sacrifice. Men with confidence can share the power to nurture and can be full partners in the human journey. For more about this, I suggest that men read Robert Bly. Another author, Carol Gilligan, is one I suggest for women, or both partners.

Besides the gender issue, I often hear complaints that have to do with mismatches between a "morning person" and an "evening person." If both partners are morning people, that is they both like to get up early, then they are evenly matched in terms of rhythms. In the same way, if you have two night people, they will both like to stay up late and sleep in in the morning.

The difficulty is in what to do when there is a mismatch. Mismatched couples commonly complain of being lonely, but there can be flexibility in their system if they are willing to work with it. Probably the best time for such a couple to do things together would be in the middle of the day, rather than early or late. An early supper hour or a late lunch would probably fit both of their schedules. Just because they are mismatched in this dimension doesn't mean that they can't be complementary to each other. First of all, they must stop criticizing each other for what the other partner's pattern is. They must get past the idea that the evening person is lazy or the morning person is boring. They just have different patterns which must be accepted, and worked with.

We need to remember that the concept of gender is basically a learned pattern. If it is learned, that means that we can look at our patterns and choose to make some changes. Now right away, some of us will point to our partner and say that he or she should be the one to change. But we need to look at our own patterns, and decide what we want to change about ourselves. In the same way, our partner needs to look at his/her own pattern, and decide what to change.

Styles of Communicating

꒜

It begins with touching. Life occurs because we touch each other.

When we no longer touch, life withers. Love is unsatisfied with distance.

Intimacy reaches its total expression when a communion of hearts becomes a bonding of bodies.

Anthony Padovano
Love and Destiny

In Michelangelo's famous painting, Adam is reaching out and touching the fingertip of God. As we float down the stream of life together, going back to God, we feel the need to communicate with each other. In this chapter, I will discuss the different styles that couples use to talk to each other. As most of us know, poor communication is the cause of a great deal of dissatisfaction in marriage. In one of my interviews with a couple, one lady said, "The only time we communicate is in the middle of the night when we bump into each other."

Miller, Nunnally, and Wackman, in their book *Alive and Aware,* describe four different styles of communication in marriage. The first style is what we might call "chit-chat." This is sociable, friendly, and playful talk. Little energy is put into the conversation by either partner, and we can waste a lot of time talking like this. It is pretty common that couples spend a lot of time in this mode. An example of it would be when we are at the grocery store and the checkout clerk says to us, "It looks like it's going to rain today." We might say, "Yes, it does." Neither of us puts much energy into the conversation; it's just a light, friendly way of relating to each other.

In the first, romantic stage of marriage, Mark and Tricia talk like this a great deal—it's a way of being with each other. The other four couples we've talked about do this also, to a certain degree. This "chit-chat" way of relating is a thinking style, but it is not really a method of communication.

The second style is when one partner tries to force his or her intention on the other. Randy and Becky frequently spoke of this style, and they came up with the analogy of putting a box of Kleenex on the table, and trying to force it to move or change. Becky laughs now about how Randy used phrases like "you should . . . you ought . . . you never . . . you always." He would use persuading and demanding to try to get what he wanted. With reference to the box of Kleenex, Randy said that Becky would do a lot of blaming, praising, and advising, and even directing it, but the box of Kleenex would never move. Of course, it wasn't the box of Kleenex, it was the other person that each partner wanted to move. Neither of them ever got the Kleenex—or the partner—to move using these methods—but a lot of bad feelings built up, and the hurt feelings came from within themselves and not from each other. This style of relating doesn't work—the box would never move—there is no magic!

Along with the words that this couple used, you could add

defending, assuming, withholding, evaluating, controlling, provoking, competing, and being unresponsive to the list. Any time we use these ways of relating, a lot of bad feelings build up, and along with these feelings comes extreme frustration. Again, this comes from within ourselves, not from our partner. Randy and Becky soon found this out, and after a period of time in their marriage, realized that many families pass this style on to their children. It doesn't work—and this couple is now making a point of not teaching their children to relate in this way. If couples fail to work this through, they soon build a wall between each other that becomes more and more insurmountable. They continue to blame each other for not changing, rather than looking at themselves.

The third style is a thinking style, which might be somewhat foreign to us—but it works. This is when a couple moves past the power stage into stability, and deeper commitment to each other. If we listen to our couples as they communicate with each other in this stage, we might hear Jerry, for instance, in discussing a decision, say to his wife Ellen: "Probably we could explore some options." Ellen might say, "Let's elaborate some more about this situation." Jack might say to his wife, "Let's talk about what we might do this weekend." Or Bev would say, "Could we search for some more options on what we might do?" Hank and Eva tended to say things like, "I was pondering this particular situation and wondering what we might do."

When we use these words—exploring, elaborating, speculating, searching, pondering, wondering, proposing, reflecting —and preface these words with "maybe . . . we might," we create "open" questions. The five couples noted that they all needed to practice using this as a means of communication— but it was clear that it worked. The couples noticed that when they tried style two, it definitely did not work!

A fourth style that Miller, Nunnally, and Wackman talked

about was the disclosing of self. This is called intimacy, which was previously discussed in this book. The difficulty with this type of disclosure about the self, the couples found, was when after one partner disclosed something, the other person would say something like, "Well, that is your problem." It's very difficult to disclose when the other person rejects the information. If this happens, the disclosing person can be hurt on a very deep level, because the feelings that the partner is disclosing are extremely sensitive.

So communication styles can vary, from those that waste time, to those that don't work, to those that do work in terms of thinking and feeling. Controlling, or style two, was a problem for three of the five couples for a time. They all had to unlearn that method. When they did, and moved to styles three and four, their relationships grew and improved.

Deborah Tannen, in her book, *You Just Don't Understand,* spoke about how two people try to build a network of friendship, minimize their differences, and somehow reach a consensus. In doing this, our five couples try to avoid the appearance of superiority, which would highlight their differences. When men and women highlight their differences, as we discussed in the previous chapter, we find that women tend to be more focused on intimacy, while men tend to focus on independence. So each couple must balance these tendencies toward intimacy and independence when they talk to each other. The women in our five couples, particularly Becky, Ellen, and Eva, tended to automatically consult their partners about a decision, asking questions like, "What do you think?" But when Jerry heard this from his wife, he assumed that he had to decide what was going to be done.

Choosing our communication style is much like going into a restaurant and picking up a menu. There are different choices that can be made from the menu. The same is true of different styles of communication. For example, Eva has a style in which she is more inclined to do what is asked of her, while her husband Hank is inclined to resist even the slightest hint that anyone would tell him what to do. If Jerry was driving down the street, and up ahead Becky was trying to pull out of a parallel parking space, Jerry would probably stop and wave at Becky, telling her to go ahead. She would probably wave back, thinking he was being nice, and proceed out into traffic. But what if Jerry was driving along and Becky's husband Randy was the one driving? If Jerry came to a stop and waved at Randy to go forward, Randy would probably wave back at him, urging him to go on. Randy would not want to be controlled or to be submissive in this situation. There can be differences in how men and women react to particular situations.

Across from my office is a playground for a grade school. It is interesting to sit and watch the boys and girls play. For instance, the boys tend to play in large groups that are very structured, with a leader who is giving orders, and trying to make these orders stick. Each game seems to have a winner and a loser, and a set of rules. Boys seem to have a lot of arguments about who is the best at whatever game they're playing. Meanwhile, the girls come out to play in smaller groups, tending to stay with their "best friends." Intimacy seems to be the key here. The girls tend to play more jump rope and other games with just one other person. Their games seem to have fewer winners and losers, and are not based as much on skill. If you listen to them very carefully, the girls on the playground don't give as many orders, but they do give suggestions. When these little boys and girls grow up and enter into marriages, each will have a certain style that they will carry into their marriage.

An example of this difference is shown in the case of Bev and Jack Black. Bev discovered that she had a lump in one of her breasts. She came home very upset about it, and was sharing her feelings with Jack about the problem. Jack replied, "Well, you should go to the hospital, and they can cut it out, so there won't

39

be any problem." Bev was concerned with communicating her feelings with Jack, and he was on another level, thinking about "fixing" the problem. In this particular case, Bev was very hurt that her husband was giving advice, and that he wasn't listening to her. Jack was operating on a thinking level, and wasn't sharing with her on a feeling level. Jack may have been offering sound advice, but to Bev he seemed very cold. Men need to be aware that women tend to share feelings—they don't necessarily want a conclusion, they just want to be heard, and they want the other person to listen and relate to them on a feeling level.

Hank also went through this about growing older. Eva stated that Hank had difficulty with the age factor, but that he eventually shared his feelings with her. When she stayed on the feeling level with him, they did a lot of intimate sharing about their fears, and this helped them to become closer.

If communication continues on a feeling level, some men might think that the woman is getting "mushy," not getting anywhere in solving the problem, even wallowing in the problem. The man might want to try to solve the problem, coming across as cold to the woman. If this happens, it is best for both parties to step back a bit, and realize that these are different communication styles, and that they are not intended to cut the other party off. Ellen and Jerry Grey came to realize that men and women sometimes communicate differently and expect different responses. Ellen especially would like to have her feelings supported, while Jerry would attack the cause behind his feelings, rather than talk about his feelings.

When I was extremely small, I noticed how my mother and a number of ladies from the neighborhood used to get together and visit. When I would go into the living room and listen to them, I always felt that they were wasting time. I realize now that I was looking at this from a man's point of view. The women were establishing intimacy, and they weren't being destructive when they talked about things that were going on in the neighborhood. This sharing of secrets is the groundwork for friendship. Very seldom were men present when the women used their form of gossip. I suppose that men might find it risky to expose their vulnerability by sharing their secrets; they might see it as an attack on their independence.

When women recall a name or an event, it is actually a sign of caring. When they do this, it draws them closer together. Men sometimes will recall an incident, as when Hank says to Eva, "I recall when you wore this particular dress." He uses it as a means of "flirting" with her.

Tricia and Mark are in the romantic stage, and both use patterns common to men and women. Tricia, in talking to Mark, attempts to build rapport with him, while Mark finds himself measuring what she is saying in competitive terms. When Mark gets into competition, and when Tricia is into rapport, they are simply using two different communication systems. Awareness of this often comes at the end of the romantic stage, when partners are starting to "see through" the illusions that were set up. This moves them into the power stage.

Jack and Hank both realized over time that their conversational styles were somewhat aggressive and competitive, and that they enjoyed a little bit of verbal combat. When their wives realized this, they were able to take it less seriously. All five couples found that when their imaginations got involved in the conversation, the combat became ritualized. The women would be puzzled by what the men were doing. Many of the men would feel rather good after a knock-down, drag-out fight, because they regarded this as a ritual form of combat, and a sign of involvement. Many of the women would feel very weary and defeated after a fight. The males tended to see a particular interaction one way, while females saw it another way.

When I talk to couples in my office, I normally ask them about their nationality. Some find this odd, but one of the things I have found is that different conversational styles that are characteristic of different nationalities can muddy the waters. One member of a couple might come from a home where a lot of conversation went on at the table—much of it overlapping, but everyone enjoying it. The other member of the couple might come from a home in which there are no interruptions, and where males are given first choice of food and are fed first, and the conversation tends to be dominated by males, with the females expected to sit back and listen.

I'm not saying that one method is correct and another wrong, but each couple does need to look at their family system and see what styles they learned. When couples talk to each other from their heads and their hearts, each needs to listen extremely carefully to the other person's style, for it is unique to them.

Several times in this chapter I have used the word "intimacy." Anthony Padovano, in his book *Love and Destiny*, defined intimacy this way:

> Intimacy is our capacity to listen to the life story of another, to hear it without judgment, to receive it without measuring it against a more ideal life. Intimacy allows me to tell my own story to someone I know will not violate it, to someone who will not force me to make a fiction of my life, to someone who will keep sacred the memory and the meaning of my identity.

Each of the couples I've discussed here is in the process of learning this responsibility, and they hope to come as close as possible to this ideal.

One of the things I've observed as I've gone around the country giving workshops is that people use words differently, and have different views of the world. My experience has been that their views can be just as valid as mine. Sometimes I have to sit back and listen. A form of communicating with a person is listening to their views and being open to their way of interpreting the world. Virginia Satir, in her book, *People Making,* talked about open and closed systems. In marriages which are closed systems, self-esteem is very low, the communication styles are indirect and unclear, and there is a lot of blaming. The rules are very set, and the marriage system is pretty chaotic. In contrast, an open system is characterized by high self-esteem, direct and clear communication, and up-to-date rules which change when they need to change. When you have an open system in marriage, there is a better chance of good communication; in a closed system, unexpressed hurts cause walls to go up, so that the other can't get too close.

Communication in marriage can be very exciting or very painful, depending on whether we can learn how to grow together and listen carefully to each other. Each couple needs to learn how to develop a style of communication that will work for their marriage.

Conflict and Forgiveness

ॐ

Here we are, two good people floating down the river of life. Both of us have a dream that life should be peaceful and harmonious, and that we will always be very nice to each other. It is especially true in a Christian dream that everything should be peaceful all the time. But our human nature enters into this, and being human, we are not above reaching across and shaking the other's boat once in a while to see if we can get a reaction.

What can we learn about ourselves from a conflictual situation? What can we learn about our relationship? First of all, the expectation that everything is supposed to go correctly all the time, without any problems, is misleading. If we use the life of Christ as an example, we see that he spent most of his life involved in resolving conflict. We humans tend to avoid conflict, or fear it. Yet even with this fear, most of us end up getting into some kind of power struggle.

When we first marry, we have this vision that everything is supposed to be perfect. Mark and Tricia, who were newly married and in the romantic stage, definitely avoided conflict, because it didn't fit in with their vision—it doesn't fit in with the idea of oneness. So they didn't deal with their differences, their struggles, and especially their aloneness before the other person. Here, religions play a big part in pushing the idea that everything is supposed to be perfect, living with God and with each other.

The first thing we have to realize about conflict is that we should trust ourselves to act or speak or think according to what we believe. By doing this we become aware of the human condition. In another way, conflict in marriage helps us discover who God is. We learn not to get so wrapped up in our own belief that we start assuming some responsibility for what we are doing in this conflict. Again, if we look at our family structure, what did we learn from our family about solving conflict? Many families just ignore conflict, pretending that there isn't a problem. Others make a lot of noise, but never resolve the issues. Mark and Tricia needed to start dealing with the fact that they each brought a different pattern into the relationship. Instead of fighting like they did in his family or her family, they needed to see what they could use as their own pattern.

If we accept that conflict is inevitable, is there room for such a thing as forgiveness? The concept of forgiveness is an uneasy one for most people. Part of the reason for this is that we tend to see things in terms of measurement. Forgiveness is simply a decision. We decide to forgive not for the other's sake, but for our own sake. If we were locked in a jail, and the bars were the feeling parts of the situation, we might pull back and hold back each time we touched those bars. So we'd stay in jail. But if we deal with the feelings, we can come up to the bars and pass through.

If we are focused on being right, we find that it is a pretty cold world out there, and that we have a pretty cold relationship. If we decide to forgive, we risk, we come up to the bars, and we walk through. In a sense, we are walking toward openness, which makes us vulnerable again to the other person.

The first step is acknowledging that there is a conflict and that we have hurt one another. We ask the person to accept us with our vulnerability. To forgive does not imply that we are right or wrong. In my workshops, I use the example that when Jesus forgives, he also forgets. Maybe we've hurt someone more than once, and we come back to Jesus and say, "I did this again, and I need your forgiveness." And Jesus says, "What?" This example always seems to amaze people, because we tend to have strings attached to our forgiveness.

In a relationship, whether it's a young couple like the Whites, who are recently married, or the Golds, who have been married for many, many years, there is a place for conflict as well as forgiveness. Conflict is a human quality which forces growth in the individual person and in the relationship. But most of us have been taught very little about conflict and forgiveness.

Dudley Weeks, in his book, *Conflict Partnership,* discussed a number of techniques that can be used to help resolve problems. First of all, we need to examine what our own needs, values, and goals are in the situation that are in conflict with the other person's. Along with this, we need to think about timing; that is, are we free of outside distractions, is it a good time to discuss this situation? If one partner is a morning person and the other is an evening person, there will have to be a special time set aside for the discussion. A reasonable amount of time is needed—squeezing it in during commercial breaks in a TV show wouldn't be adequate. It's important to have a calm, quiet physical environment—so that the partners can sit down and figure out "where are we at?" with the issue.

I sometimes advise people to plan their opening comments, to say something like, "I have very strong feelings, and I know you probably do too, about this, and I'd like for the two of us to look at some options." If I have a couple in my office who have a disagreement, the first thing I always do is to try to get them to clarify and understand what the conflict is about. Many times it is as if the partners are each on a different "frequency" on the CB. If one is on Channel 19 and the other on Channel 15, there isn't going to be much communication. But if we give the other person time to answer, and if we don't interrupt, then we can clarify things. We might even want to take a watch and say, "for this amount of time you'll express your needs, then I'll express my needs."

I always ask people to listen to what their own bodies are telling them—the heartbeat, sweating, and so on. Sometimes we need to try to separate out the one issue that is being fought about, and put other things aside. Sometimes we need to listen to our own internal voices, to hear what they are saying, and to sort out what we want to follow up on. One of the best techniques is to speak only for ourselves and our own feelings, never about the partner. If we start name-calling and talking about how our partner's family "always does things this way," we've lost it. Unrealistic demands and threats will get us nowhere, as will labels and attacking our partner's vulnerabilities.

Stressing positives will get us much further than focusing on negatives. It's especially important for each partner to take responsibility for his or her contribution to the conflict. Doing this may make us feel vulnerable, but stepping forward and taking some responsibility will help the situation work out better.

This human tendency to reach out and shake our partner's boat can be done in playfulness, but we must be careful that this playfulness does not evolve into a conflict where we hurt our partner. It is all too easy to hurt our partner emotionally, psychologically, and spiritually.

Just as we sometimes hurt our marriage partner, we have tensions in our Christian community, which we often try to avoid—but this avoidance makes us uncomfortable. Just like Jesus did in his life, we should stay with it—after every conflict there is always the resurrection!

Types of Marriages

୧๛

There are different types of marriage systems, and they all seem to work in their own ways; difficulties seem to arise when one person comes from one type of family and the other comes from another type of family. When they try to put the two systems together, they might have problems, although the systems might be perfectly good in themselves. The different systems may have different goals and objectives, or different standards, but they do work.

This type of relationship is like a circle with a center. The person in the center tends to think that he or she is in charge of the whole system, and the other person revolves around the outside and picks up all the pieces. It is questionable whether the person in the center or the one on the outside is really in charge. This is like the marriages of many of our grandparents, marriages which had strictly defined jobs. An example would be a husband working outside and the wife working inside, cleaning the house, cooking, and sewing. Both work hard all day, and then when they sit down for the evening meal, the wife serves the meal to the husband and children. After dinner, the husband reads the paper while the wife cleans the kitchen. In this type of situation, there is little need for communication skills. The arrangement works as long as neither partner wants to

Number One: The Center of the Universe Type

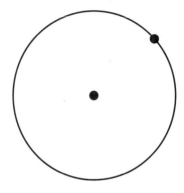

Figure 1.

change the situation or leave it. But if one partner challenges the other, the balance no longer holds.

The Green's marriage was a two-people type. The two people are like two overlapping circles, with the overlapping area representing the sharing part of the relationship. There is a significant need for communication in this type of system. This type of relationship is the kind which many people got into in recent years, a relationship where much more sharing is expected than in the past. For instance, the husband and wife probably both work, and when they come home, there are common chores to be done. They probably divide the chores according to who likes to do what. If the wife doesn't like cooking, for example, but doesn't mind doing laundry, then she ends up with the laundry. Communication skills are needed so that partners can negotiate a balance between themselves. Difficulties can arise when one partner is used to one style, and the other to another.

Virginia Clemente, a marriage and family therapist, uses triangles to illustrate the different positions that people will

Number Two: The Two-People Type

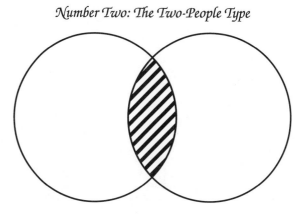

Figure 2.

take in their relationships. There are three different positions in the triangle—ourselves at the top, followed by our spouse. The third part is others, that is, the kids and jobs. We relate back and forth in terms of the triangle. First of all, we take care of ourselves, then our spouse, then the children and jobs. Difficulty comes in this system when one partner puts something between themselves and his or her spouse. For example, the Greys had a problem in their marriage when Jerry, who was a farmer, put work between himself and his wife. He worked for very long hours, and Ellen, his wife, was pushed out of the picture. Ellen responded by putting the children between the two. So the two of them had difficulties for quite a while until they put their priorities back in order.

The upside down triangle is when we put ourselves at the bottom. Becky, of the Green family, was an example of this. She tended to "take care" of everyone in the family, neglecting herself, and carrying the weight of the world on her shoulders. Carrying on like this creates anger and resentment, and Becky needed to get her priorities in order. She had to learn to take

Number Three: The Pyramid Type

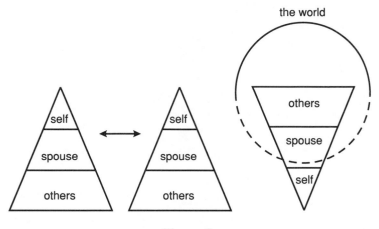

Figure 3.

care of herself physically, emotionally, psychologically, spiritually, and in her relationships.

This type applies to just about all marriages. It is a way of charting family relationships, in which male members are represented as squares and females as circles. A line is drawn between the two, and the year of the marriage is written down. From that line, the children are drawn in, with oldest child on the left and continuing to the right. Each time the child is labeled as boy or girl. If a child is stillborn, or if one of the family members died, an "x" is drawn through that particular circle or square. The marriage system is drawn as a circle around the couple. Another circle represents the family system including the children, and a third circle represents work, play, church, and other activities. There is a door next to the father and mother, through which each can go out to their friendship relationships. Each partner in the marriage needs friendships, because the marriage won't satisfy all of their needs.

Number Four: The Genogram Type

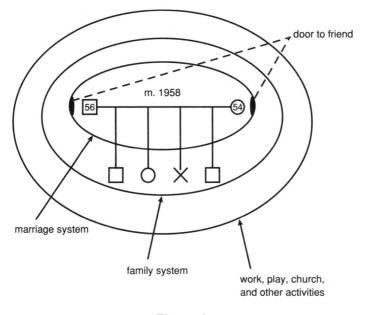

Figure 4.

In the inner circle of the marriage, intimacy is needed between the two partners, which is shared only between the two of them. If a partner goes outside of that circle emotionally or sexually, it violates that marriage system. The second thing that is in that circle is conflict resolution. That is, the two of them set up some way of resolving conflicts, which they have learned from their families of origin, or through readings. This diagram can be expanded into a very large genogram, to see exactly where we are in our family system, where we came from, what nationalities are involved, and what traits are passed on through the family, such as humor, discipline, and so on.

How We Build Relationships

ॐ

When we are floating down the river of life, each in our own boat, we set up relationships with other people in different ways. Relationships are how marriages start, and how two partners become involved with each other.

Virginia Clemente uses a drawing to describe a marriage pattern, which is a circle with diagonal lines drawn through it. On different parts of the circle are opposite words, like strong-weak, angry-loving—any set of words can be used as long as they express opposites. Each partner needs to develop his or her own circle, with all the parts. It is up to each of us to develop it. Take, for example, the situation of a strong, angry football player, whom we could think of as half a circle, falling in love with a weak, loving cheerleader, another half of a different circle. If they get married, each bringing half of a circle to the marriage, the marriage system will not run. You have to have two wheels for a bicycle, and you need two complete persons for a marriage to work. Each partner, the husband and the wife, must develop his or her own part of the circle, so that at some time in the relationship, a partner can be strong, and other times weak. Each must learn to be angry at times, and to be loving at other times. We might say that we don't want to be weak, but we are weak at times so that our partner may be strong at times. Marriages take two complete people to work. All of us need to work on those parts of the circle that are incomplete in our personality. This takes time. The more we expect our partner to carry part of the circle, the more difficulties we will have.

Another image for building a relationship would be a glass of water with food coloring in it. This glass would be much lighter in color at the top, and darker on the bottom. In a relationship, we relate to each other on a number of different levels. Starting from the top we have five levels. These are values, how we talk, our feelings for each other, the relational, and the physical aspects of the relationship. In the glass of water, draw an imaginary line between the talking and feeling part. When you look at your partner through the glass, the water would be cloudy on the bottom, less cloudy in the middle, and clear on top. This is to illustrate the difficulty we may have when we look at our partner, when we fall in love, and we are involved in the relational, the feeling, and the touching parts of the relationship. There is nothing wrong with this, as long as we remain committed to our values. But when a relationship stays in this bottom area, when we look through the water we will see a very cloudy image, or we will only see what we want to see. As a result, we won't engage with our partner in the value area—we won't ask questions of each other such as: "What do you want out of a relationship?" "What do you expect out of a relationship?" If we marry and remain on the bottom part of the glass, it might be fine for awhile, but usually one partner will want to go up above the line. The wife might say to the husband, "Honey, let's talk," and the husband says, "What??" It is as if they don't want to go above the line at the same time. This can cause great difficulties. It is easier to build a relationship starting with the values and talking. If we build up a friendship first, that friendship can develop greater feelings, relational qualities, and touching aspects, which can be integrated into the relationship according to each person's values. But if we start at the bottom and try to clarify later on, it becomes very difficult. If our number-one value in a relationship is security, for example, but our partner relegates that to number nine, we might end up fighting over that for the rest of our lives. If we had been friends first, we would have known our partner's position on that issue long before. Feelings, relational issues, and touching are powerful forces which attract us to one another, and it is easy to substitute these for talking about our values. Sadly, in many cases, people find that—years after their marriage—they don't like each other. This is a clear danger in a marriage when the values have not been clarified at the beginning.

The psychologist Carl Jung said that each person has a shadow part of the unconscious. Therefore, each of two people who are in a relationship has a shadow. When we stand in the sun, there is a shadow behind us, and similarly, the part of our personality with which we are uncomfortable stands behind us. This doesn't mean that the shadow is bad, but it contains parts of us that have, for whatever reason, been buried in the unconscious. Things about ourselves that our parents, or our teachers, or our church said were bad are put away in the shadow. Over the years we bury a lot of information in that shadow.

The shadow has a contrasexual part. This means that a male person will have female qualities in the shadow, which may be good or bad. There would be good female qualities that women have in general, such as caring, warmth, and emotional expression, and bad qualities that women have in general, such as being extremely opinionated. The female who is married to this person would have male qualities buried in her shadow. There might be good qualities that males have in general, such as being strong and solving problems. There would also be bad qualities attributed to males, such as moodiness.

When two people are talking to each other, feelings can be shared back and forth. An example of this is where Hank and Eva share with each other their experience of a beautiful sunset. Next we can describe the relationship that each partner has with his or her own shadow. We are often uncomfortable with the shadow, and that discomfort is projected onto the other partner. This means that we see the parts of ourselves which we can't accept in ourselves, as being situated in our partner. Hank laughs about the fact that he is uncomfortable about himself being bossy and does not deal with it, but instead claims that Eva is bossy. The next step is one in which the partner's shadow reacts to the other partner's shadow. When we get married, we tend to see the contrasexual part of the other person's shadow. That is, the male sees in the female the male qualities that he really likes, and the female sees in the male the female qualities she likes. Each identifies with the qualities of the other's shadow. This happens in the romantic stage. This projection that goes back and forth will break at some later stage.

What happens is that we get into the negative parts of the shadow, and we start fighting. Suppose Jerry, the husband of the family, comes home and he is very moody. He doesn't talk about it—it is his way of dealing with something within himself. He sits there grumbling, and Ellen, his wife, sees this, and the negative part of her shadow interacts with this moodiness. She might act out her shadow by being very opinionated (her way of getting distance). These opinions may be from something she had read or heard at church, or from her friends; being opinionated would be one way that she would keep people from being too close to her. Now, if Jerry is very moody and Ellen is very opinionated, their interaction is like throwing gasoline on a fire—Jerry grumbles, and Ellen comes in and says, "What's wrong with you?" All of a sudden there is a huge fight and they wonder, "My Lord, we are just about destroying each other! What is going on?"

Fights like this, in which the contrasexual shadow parts of ourselves are engaged with each other, can be extremely mean and hurtful. Many times the fights we have have more to do with the relationships that we as individuals have between our heads and our hearts than they have to do with the other person. As we travel down the stream of life and enter into the second half of life, conflicts between the head and the heart often develop. When the conflict becomes too great, we might project it onto our partner. The results of this can be frightening, and if it is not dealt with, it can develop into a mid-life crisis.

The element of time is an important part in a relationship. We have 24 hours in a day, and how do we divide up our time? One part is individual time. These are the times when we sit outside, do what we need to do, go fishing, or just sit and watch television—doing whatever we choose to do individually. Another part is optimum time—when we share time with a significant other. If we consider our partners to be important, we need to spend time with them and do things with them. We don't have to spend every moment with them, because that would be overwhelming. But we need to spend time with our partner, quality time when we are not tired or distracted. The third part would be diffused time. This is when we are sitting there, watching a show on television, and at the same time thinking about things we have to do, and then thinking about something else, and something else. We might think about a fight we had, or some shopping we need to do, or about something else that comes to mind—and by the time we come back to the television set, the show is over. In diffused time, the mind tends to wander all over the place, and if we have too much of it, we might think we're "going crazy." But this isn't the same as "being crazy." It's one of those things that, if unchecked tends to occur more and more often, and that might have a negative impact on our relationship. We can stop the wandering by simply bringing our attention back to the TV show, or whatever we wish to focus our attention on.

I brought up the element of time here because it is important to realize that we need to not only spend time with each other, but to spend time alone so that we can get our own individual act together. Part of doing this involves dealing with the shadow parts of ourselves—taking a look at what is in the shadow, what is bothering us, what we've hidden from ourselves. Looking at the shadow takes courage, honesty, and time —it is a lifetime process. But it is ultimately rewarding, because along with the negative aspects which we must deal with, we will find all kinds of "unpolished gems"—parts of our personality that we can transform into things that are worth much to us. On top of that, we can improve the quality of our relationships by learning not to project our problems onto our partner.

Synchronicity

In his writings, Carl Jung discussed synchronicity as the attraction of opposites. This is a story based on opposites.

As we float down the river of life on our way back to God, many times we are attracted to what is exactly the opposite. On the left side of the river is "Oneness." We can think of this as the time when we were in our mother's womb. At the beginning, we were warm and comfortable, were totally dependent, and had all our needs met under perfect conditions. But as we grew to six, seven, eight months, we started kicking, wanting more room—every mother can tell us about this. At this point, we are trying to move across the river to what is called "separateness." When we are born, we have that separateness—we are becoming independent, and all of our needs can't be instantly met. It was warm in the womb, but now it's sometimes cold, and we sometimes have to wait to be taken care of. So we go from one extreme to another.

As newborns, we probably didn't know that we were separate—we thought that we were everything and that everything was us. But then we'd swing an arm around, and hit ourselves in the nose—and we'd slowly learn that there are things "out there" that affect us. We learned to mold ourselves closely to our mother's body as she held us—but there was another quality we had, called "bridging." We would bridge, or arch our back. We can see that now, when we hold a baby—all of a sudden the baby will kick out, wanting to be separate.

Later, as we sit on our mother's lap, we start trusting others whom she trusts, and we reach out to hold someone's knee, and we want to go "over there." We might have oneness with one parent, and we want to go over to the other. But once we arrive over there, we want to go right back. We can see that when we watch kids—they are always moving, back and forth, going some place, coming back. If a small child crawls around a corner and can't see the parent, those little cries of distress we hear are the baby saying to the parent, "Are you still there? I can't see you!" At that age, the child can't imagine that the parent is still there, around the corner. So at this stage we have oneness, but we are trying to separate, and there is a lot of anxiety involved.

One day we are packed up and sent to Grandma and Grandpa's house to stay overnight. Now we are really going to have some separateness. At first, in the car on the way there, it is a big adventure and everything is wonderful. But then when we realize that we're going to be left at Grandma and Grandpa's house, there is much screaming and yelling! So we want that separation but we aren't too sure of ourselves. As we grow a little older, about seven or eight, we might make a few friends in the neighborhood, at first just to be able to get out of the house. Then, because we still aren't too sure of ourselves, we begin doing whatever our group is doing, and feeling pain if we aren't included. But we are separating more from our parents at this time.

When we get into adolescence, our primary task is to make the transition to adulthood and leave home—but we don't always do it in a comfortable way. We usually do it in one of three ways: 1) We were so focused on getting out of the house that we ran out in the street, not knowing where we were going, just wanting to get away; 2) We backed out of the house, criticizing our parents and siblings, accusing them of not knowing anything about life or love or relationships. Our energy was still focused on the house in this case; or 3) We left sideways—that is, when we got out into the street, we knew which way we were going, but we also knew where the house was. This is probably the best way to do it. Everybody needs to leave home emotionally, and in the process of getting this separateness, we are better equipped for new relationships. Many of us accomplished this by going into the military, or moving across town, or even to another city. But we might not have resolved the emotional issues involved with this separation.

Then, as we continued down the stream of life, we met somebody, and all of a sudden we fell in love. Falling in love was like perfect oneness—like being back in the womb. We feel as if all of our needs are being met again. We get married, and ride off in a car—we're both looking out the window together, looking toward the future, feeling as if we are one. In a week or two, we're back, and we are looking out of our own separate windows. So we have our separateness again.

We try to resolve this separateness/oneness problem in two ways. One way is "splitting" the emotion. This means that when we fight, we try to resolve the issue of oneness and separateness by saying that "I am all good, and you are all bad." These fights hurt us so deeply because of the fantasy that our relationship is supposed to be perfect, like it was in the womb. So our dream is that it should all be perfect, and when it is not, we tend to blame our partner.

A second way in which we try to solve this problem is instead of becoming totally dependent or totally independent, we work at becoming interdependent. This is a philosophy or an attitude about life in which we realize that we will spend the entire journey of life, as we move down the stream back to God, dealing with this issue.

We can choose to deal with the separation/oneness issues

in three steps. In the first step, we have to deal with ourselves (the "Me" part). On one end of that continuum is loneliness, when we are sitting looking out the window—but the windows are all mirrors, reflecting back inward. On the other end is solitude, or peace of heart. When we are comfortable with ourselves, when we have a certain degree of self-esteem, we can feel good about the activities we do as an individual. We build our self-esteem by giving ourselves credit for the things we do, by "stroking" ourselves in a positive manner. Whether we are doing laundry, or driving, or carrying out any of our daily tasks, if we tell ourselves, "I did a good job on this . . . I did a good job on that," it becomes a habit. After awhile, we start feeling good about ourselves and our accomplishments.

So we must first deal with ourselves before we can turn to others to build positive relationships. If my self-esteem is low, or if I am lonely, I am going to be hostile to others. I might strike out at others, even at my partner in marriage. But if I feel comfortable with myself, if I have peace of heart, and solitude, I will offer hospitality to others, I will be nice to them. On this continuum, we have hostility and hospitality in dealing with others.

So basically, the quality of our relations depends on ourselves first, then on our partner or neighbor, and from there to God. If we are lonely and hostile to our partner, then we will become disillusioned. We might ask, where is this God who allows all the suffering in the world and all the evil that is going on? But if we have peace of heart and are comfortable with our partner, chances are we will be comfortable with God. We're able to speak to God through prayer, and we can just sit there and listen to God.

In the last continuum with God, we have disillusionment and prayer. As we move along our growth pattern from me, to you, back to God, we are bound to have a certain amount of pain. This pain is closely related to our growth. At all times, I think, we and our partners need to have a safe space, where we can call "time out." We just sit at that position, and let our partner carry us for awhile. But ultimately we can't expect our partner to take us on the journey of life back to God. That's our own responsibility.

These concepts were put together with another therapist, Leon Haverkamp, a social worker. As we worked on it, we tried to figure out a process of life and we came up with this one. The three steps—me, you, and God—are just the reverse of the commandments—love yourself, your neighbor, and God. Because we are human, we must work with our humanness—building our self-esteem and our relationships to others. We might want to try to go directly to God—and we can, if we choose the life of a mystic. But for most of us, we must go through our partner, our neighbor, our community—our relationships with others. I think that our partner must also be working toward growth, toward going back to God, for our journey to be successful.

In marriage, we often see the attraction of opposites. Married people, for example, have a strong desire to be single. Meanwhile, I see in my office single people who are very unhappy with themselves because they feel they should be married. They, too, want to be on the other side of the street. But the answer isn't in whether we are married or single, it's in how we deal with the process of going back to God.

The Wall

Their wedding picture mocked them from the table,
these two whose minds no longer touched each
        other.
They lived with such a heavy barricade between them
that neither battering ram of words or artilleries of
        touch
could break it down.

Somewhere, between the oldest child's first tooth
        and the
youngest daughter's graduation they lost each other.
Throughout the years, each slowly unraveled
that tangled ball of string called self,
and as they tugged at stubborn knots,
each hid his searching from the other.
Sometimes she cried at night
and begged the whispering darkness
to tell her who she was.
He lay beside her, snoring like a hibernating bear,
unaware of her winter.

Once, after they had made love,
he wanted to tell her

how afraid he was of dying,
but, fearing to show his naked soul,
he spoke instead about
the beauty of her breasts.

She took a course in modern art,
trying to find herself in colors
splashed upon a canvas,
and complained to other women
about men who were insensitive.

He climbed into a tomb called the office,
wrapped his mind in a shroud of paper figures
and buried himself in customers.

Slowly, the wall between them rose,
cemented by the mortar of indifference.
One day, reaching out to touch each other,
they found a barrier they could not penetrate,
and, recoiling from the coldness of the stones,
each retreated from the struggle on the other side.

For when love dies,
it is not a moment of angry battle,
nor when fiery bodies lose their heat.
It lies, panting, exhausted . . .
expiring at the bottom of the wall
it could not scale.

—Unknown

This poem signifies brokenness as it exists in all relationships. In a relationship, for example, the husband might put out
a few stones when he feels upset, or hurt, or angry, and he just

leaves them there. The wife might put out three or four bricks of her own when she feels angry or upset, and she leaves them there. The stones that the husband put out and the bricks that the wife put out don't amount to much at first, until the wall starts growing. After awhile, the wall might be getting pretty high—and that's when the real problem starts—when the wall is so high that the partners can't see each other.

The husband might look across the wall and see the wife's bricks, and holler at her about them. Meanwhile, the wife looks at all the husband's stones, and criticizes him because of them. But basically, nothing happens. The wall continues to grow as each partner expresses more and more frustration.

The only way to stop the wall is to start taking down our own bricks or stones. If we are on the brick side, we must stop trying to get our partner to remove the stones, and start taking away some of our own bricks. Our partner, on the other side, must start taking away some of the stones. This is basically what happens in counseling. The best thing to do if we start getting into difficulty in a relationship is to talk to somebody before the wall gets too big. The wall can be taken down, but we must answer "yes" to the question, "Am I willing to take away my own bricks or stones?" There is some risk involved in doing this, but if we do it, there is ultimately less fear in the marriage, as the wall comes further down. The wall is common to all marriages, and needs to be worked at, just like weeding in the garden. We must keep up our marriages, as we do our gardens; if we keep the wall down, we will be able to keep our partner in view, and all will go much better.

The wall tells us about the fears that we have. Everyone has fears, but most of us do not share those fears with others, because we are afraid that we will be laughed at. When couples hide their fears from each other, they let the fears become part of the wall—they become the structure in-between the stones and the bricks, the mortar that holds the wall together. When we share a fear, and express it to someone who is safe, such as our partner or a counselor, the fear loses its power in the subconscious, because we have shared some of the psychic energy that is tied to that fear.

If the fear is left in the subconscious, all of the thoughts and feelings that have been stored in the subconscious since we were tiny babies will work on the fear, and it becomes larger and larger, thus enhancing the wall. So, sharing the fear with a partner can simplify some of the problems. It can't make the fear go away, but it can lessen it.

As I sit here by my desk looking out the window at nature across the street, I see many different colors: greens, browns, some reds on the building, tans, silver, different shades of grey, light blue in the sky, many different hues of beautiful colors. I see very few solid blacks and solid whites, and the same is true in a relationship of marriage. There are very few feelings that are completely black or white; there are different shades of different colors. By sharing some of the happy shades, the brighter colors, or by sharing some of the darker shades, the sadder colors, we paint a picture of our marriage. Marriage isn't all bright colors; it isn't all sad colors. Like looking at nature, if you look at your partner, you will see many, many different shades of color. The same is true of feelings. Feelings don't make our marriages good or bad; it is what we do with those feelings that counts.

As long as we keep some flexibility with our feelings, keeping a balance of the good times and the times that aren't so good, the walls that we build up between us will tend to stay low. Even though we sometimes get angry, and build the wall back up, we will later forgive and remove some stones and bricks; it is a process of removing and putting on, but always in the end removing something.

Therefore, flexibility is important in helping the wall to slowly come down. This coming down would result from each partner putting energy into what can be changed. If our side of the wall is stones, then we should work on the stones; if our partner's side of the wall is bricks, then let him or her work on the bricks. We must give up control, of trying to change the other's patterns. We have a right to express disagreement if we don't like some pattern of our partner's, but if we are constantly talking about their pattern, we are wasting energy. If we work on our own patterns, we will get results from wanting to change things, we will get something out of our anger. It is almost like magic.

If we sat down and looked across the room at a potted plant, and told our partner: "You can do anything you want, direct, control, yell, holler at that plant, but make it go up in the air." We would say that our partner couldn't do that, that that would be magic. But we also can't make our partner go up in the air. We have a right to express differences, but if we are constantly focused on the differences, we should shift our attention to the positive. As with children, if we encourage our partner, they will usually change and proceed to do what they should do. Walls are hard, and walls are cold—the best solution with any wall is to keep it as low as possible, plant lots of flowers around it, and use it as a decoration.

Humor

ॐ

We as adults need to keep humor in our relationships and our marriage. This humor needs to be on a very positive level. There are a number of different ways to do this; the five couples we've spoken about talked to me about some of the patterns they've used.

Ellen Gray said that whenever her husband gets too serious about a subject, she breaks into "Row, row, row your boat." It's a signal for Jerry to lighten up a little bit. It is important for humor to be kept positive; negative humor can be very destructive. An example of this would be if a group of women were meeting, and one said that she had "half a mind to marry Bill." One of the other ladies would reply, "That is all it would take if you marry him."

Mark, in his new relationship with Tricia, said that they looked at cartoons together. They especially liked to rent or buy certain old movies to play on the VCR. They found some of the silent movies extremely humorous. Some videotapes of funny situations that happened in one's family can provide a great deal of positive humor.

Jack and Bev Black were particularly noted for getting special birthday, Christmas, or Easter cards for each other. Each would spend hours looking for a card before a holiday or other day that was special for their partner. There was much humor and enjoyment that came from this; they kept the cards and shared many laughs over the ideas they had come up with over the years.

When Becky Green would throw a party or have a special gathering in her home, she would set the table with all her fine china for her children or adult guests. She would always put something unique on the table as a centerpiece. Instead of flowers, her guests and family would find a tennis shoe or something like that. There was always a lot of guessing and humor about what she would use next.

We all tend to take life pretty seriously at times, and there are times when we should do so. But there are other times when we should look at the situation and say, "Well, what would it be like twenty years from now?" Maybe it's not as serious as we now think it is. All families have funny stories, as do marriages. If people are playful and sincere, sharing them with each other brings us closer together.

After many years of marriage, Eva Gold says, she and Hank finally bought their second bottle of red hot sauce for the Frigidaire, which she says is evidence that their marriage is lasting! She would ask, how many bottles of red hot sauce have you bought for *your* marriage?

Hank also has that important ability to laugh at himself when he makes a mistake. Now that he is older, his children and grandchildren seem to enjoy that. It gives them permission not to be perfect.

We can each add different things to our marriages. Sometimes I suggest that people buy each other what I call "crazy gifts." These are funny little "off the wall" items to give to each other at unexpected times. Another example would be to do things just a little bit differently than usual. For instance, having an April Fool's cookout in the backyard, but with everything backwards—dinner would start with dessert, and work in reverse order. Or, we can put humorous presents under each others' pillows—at a particular time when the relationship needs a little lightening up. Some families have told me that they keep Polaroid snapshots of family members and friends, with humorous titles underneath them.

In God's family, there is the story of when we all die and go back to God, the first thing St. Peter asks us at the gate is whether we want the smoking or non-smoking section.

We as adults can stimulate our sense of wonder, and just as children do, we can approach the world with a sense of wonder and curiosity. This can be developed with practice. I once read that adults have about five or six basic facial expressions, but children have as many as forty or fifty. Maybe each of us, as a couple, needs to stand in front of a mirror and practice making different faces, and seeing which ones can stretch our imaginations a little bit.

Hank and Eva stated that since they have become grandparents, they gather many jokes from the *New Yorker* and other magazines, and send them to their children or their grandchildren. It is a great way to stay connected to different members of the family.

Humor should have an important role to play in our lives, and sometimes it can lighten up a relationship, or lighten us up as individuals. We all need to spend some time being happy with ourselves and our partner. Humor helps us to do this—and maybe you need to go to the Frigidaire and check to see whether you need another bottle of red hot sauce!

Love as Mystery

We as couples can look at the stars and the universe as we float along in our boats. Just as we feel the pull of gravity on the earth, likewise in marriage we feel pulls when we fall in love or are in love. As we express caring and connectedness with each other, our love wakes us up to the thrills and hurts we can give each other. These pulls help bring us alive.

If we love another person, we care for that person, and we give of ourselves. Caring can open us up to hurt, which we deal with by putting up our wall and withdrawing. This is part of what we feel with the heart.

This pulling and pushing is normal with anything we love, whether it is activities, hope, memories, friends, our belief system, or feelings. Our feelings are signs of our loving. Even when we feel hurt because of loss or bereavement, our feeling comes from the absence of love, which is a sign of how much we loved.

So, there is a mystery in our loving, for it is more than just saying "yes" to our partner. There is a freedom of love, but something creeps into that freedom and changes it. This is what Gerald May, in his book, *The Awakened Heart,* calls addiction. Our passion or energy becomes "nailed" to someone or something, and we develop attachments. Then we expect some gratification from our attachments, a situation which limits our freedom, since we are dependent on the other person to behave the way we think they should. Extreme forms of this kind of attachment could be called bondage; our love has changed from unconditional to conditional.

The Blacks had difficulties with this, and came to realize that they had to give each other more unconditional love. The more they insisted on an addictive attachment, the closer they came to physical and emotional violence in their relationship. By allowing each other some space, they did better with their relationship. This space and freedom allowed them to share their feelings.

The difference is between attachment of binding desire and that of honoring desire. On the one hand, we have love that makes one a slave, and on the other, we have love that is freely given. Ideally, we would want our love to be like the ocean—with the romance flowing back and forth, between freedom and attachment. Many times this can create some exciting confusion.

Another part of the mystery of love is the growing, struggling, and trying to perfect the relationship, as compared to leaving things stable. All couples need to preserve the status quo at times and to rest, but when the stress gets strong, some couples turn to the addiction process of attachment. So it is important to grow and expand; sometimes we choose safety by pulling back, and other times we choose growth to expand our boundaries.

If addiction now limits our freedom, we can still make another choice. In making choices, risk is always involved—the risk of getting hurt by caring.

Mystery will always be there between these two pulls, and our hearts will find it exciting or painful—the difference between growing or pulling back.

The Glue

So far, we've discussed values, talking, feelings, attraction to each other, and touching in relationships. We haven't talked about spirituality and sexuality. When I discuss these topics, I'd like for us to think of them in terms of wholeness. The word "wholeness" and "holiness" come from the same Greek word; thus when we talk about the five patterns discussed earlier, we need to think of the spiritual and sexual aspects as part of these patterns.

How does a young couple, married only a few months, get to be like the Golds, who have been married for forty years? How do Randy and Becky, or Tricia and Mark, manage to get to the stage that Hank and Eva are in? I believe that each of us travels along our own path, or, to use the metaphor we've used earlier, we float along in our own river. Sometimes we have a plan as to how we're going to negotiate our progress; at other times we have no particular intention of what we want to do. Sometimes the river allows us a glimpse of our route or destination; other times we feel that we are just meandering; at still other times, we'll reach a point where we say, "Aha! something important is happening." Spiritual growth is part of our overall pattern of development and as we develop our pattern, so our partner has to develop his or her own pattern.

So what is spirituality in terms of growth? Spiritual growth is concerned with companionship—with God, and with our partner. With both God and our partner, we must establish a certain balance of being active, on the one hand, and not doing anything, on the other. To express these active and passive parts involves a certain openness and vulnerability. We develop this openness by sharing in certain ways.

At first there are many differences, and we feel as if we are climbing a steep hill or mountain. We may start off with different paths. Because there are so many choices and different ways to go, we may find many things in our relationship about which we disagree. We might take paths which are not successful; in our trip down the river, we may choose to go through a rapid, or a whirlpool, and our partner may choose not to. This whirlpool may be growth-producing, or it may not. Later, we might cross over a still pond, which reflects to us things which we may have been familiar with before, but we might see them in a new way, seeing aspects that we have previously missed.

When we do this, it is an expression of the spiritual part of us. Spiritual knowing is always evolving. In our relationship, we become more aware of who we are, what our needs are, and in doing this we become more aware of our partner, and start to accept them as they are, rather than trying to change them to what we want them to be.

Intimacy can begin first of all in terms of spirituality—making contact with ourselves, and then with our partner. As an example, recently I visited a relative, who told me about a group of ten women who, when they were first married, agreed to get together every Monday afternoon at 4 PM, once a month to have coffee. Thirty-five years later they are still doing this, laughing, and having a good time. Over the years, intimacy and trust has developed in this group, and the group has become spiritually connected with each other; their paths in life have become similar.

Over time, in our relationship, we will stand back and look at the path we are taking down the river. We might experience this as a thinking process at one time, and as an intuitive process at another time. We know when we feel in harmony as we are floating down the river together. To have spiritual wholeness, we need to see reality as it is—in the ways in which we are connected in an integral way to everything. So if wholeness or holiness means being connected to everything, then we must be connected to ourselves, to our partner, and to the natural world around us. We need to recognize, however, that we are different. If we see a tree standing along the river bank, and say, "I would rather be that tree, it is rooted, and it seems to know exactly what it is doing," we know that that tree has to stay on the river bank and cannot move on. A human being, for his or her own spiritual growth, has a right to move on.

As we are floating along, we might not be in contact with our river. If we are constantly throwing stuff overboard from our boat, and adding filth and poison fumes to the air, we are not connected to the earth in the proper way.

Earlier, I mentioned about expanding our boundaries to bring about our growth. To do this, we sometimes have to suffer. As human beings, we have to be very gentle with ourselves. There is an old Buddhist saying, "Don't push the river." This means that we shouldn't be fanatics about our growth or our guilt about certain attachments. As we float along the river, we should keep in mind that it could be dangerous to be too rigid in our approach to our progress. We need flexibility as individuals, in our relationships, and in our spirituality.

I believe that it often helps couples to take two-minute vacations. A two-minute vacation is when we stop what we are doing, go out and sit on the front steps or in a chair someplace, and just quiet ourselves down. We can look out the window, or watch a bird fly, or an ant crawl across the lawn. As we sit there, we begin to quiet ourselves, finding out what is going on inside.

Then we can allow God to speak into our system. If we are noisy and carrying on all the time, our partner can't get close to us—because he or she can't get through all the confusion to reach us. So, as part of our spiritual practice, it is important for us to quiet ourselves. Many parents say that this is not possible —but I always say, you have a bathroom—sit down and lock the door!

Married couples don't live in a controlled environment like a monastery, where they would be taught to be quiet and listen to one another. We often have to consciously build quiet-ness into our lives. I have a friend who loves to bake bread. This is her quiet time. Everything is still and peaceful as she kneads the bread, and at that time, making the bread is all she has to do. So she lives for that particular moment.

There are a few things that get in the way of a couple's spiritual progress. These are the five "P's": possessions, power, prestige, profit, and pleasure. All of these need to be kept in moderation; if they are out of control, our spiritual life tends to be out of control, too.

Our spiritual life takes a certain amount of discipline and dedication. The discipline is a letting go and waiting; the final timing is not ours to determine. We simply need to quiet our-selves. Sometimes when we sit on the steps together and watch a sunset, we can have a very close, intimate experience with our spouse. The intimacy that happens at that particular moment is spiritual growth—happening between the two of us, or be-tween us and God, or our Higher Power. Thinking on this, I am reminded of a story I once wrote about a flower that was in a pot in a large living room. There was a large window right next to the flower, but because there was a shade on the window that was always drawn, the flower was dying. So the flower did not experience the warmth and the caring and the growth that it could have received from the sun, if only the shade had been opened. Sometimes we sit in front of a window with the shade pulled down like this, and we complain that God, or the Higher Power, is not helping us in a particular situation. We carry on complaining, but we do not assume the responsibility for pulling the shade up, and sitting in the sunlight! If we don't pull up that shade, we tend to have boredom in our relationship. We act like children sitting in the middle of a room, surrounded by toys, complaining that there is nothing to play with.

As we get older, it is our responsibility to reach out and make certain choices in life. The choices we make open up a range of possibilities as our spiritual path widens and grows. When we do this, boredom disappears. Boredom seems to be a big issue for some couples after they are married for awhile. They say, "Is this all there is?" But it is our own responsibility to reach out and put some new growth into that pattern. That new growth tends to be in the form of spiritual growth—which we can experience when we relax with the idea that we are married —and that we can make it work.

One of the nicest things that we can do to make spiritual connections with each other in our families is to set up rituals. These could be, for example, birthday parties or special dinners, or the way that we say prayers at a particular meal, or in the evening, when we may read the Bible together. Rituals tend to draw us closer to one another, and we will find ourselves feeling comfortable and trusting with each other.

I give the people who come to my office a small rock, and I ask them to put this rock somewhere special—their quiet place, their place of growth. We all need to have such a place. In our journey of life, that rock becomes a spiritual treasure, and it can be used by our partner and ourselves to help us communicate. We can put it out in a special place. That means that we want to talk to our partner, we want to share something. But we need to do this very gently and carefully. Spirituality can help us slowly move from selfishness to consideration, and then finally to love. If we engage with our partner on this basis, we can bring about radical changes in our relationship, ones which bring about growth.

We are often a little uncomfortable with ourselves, and we want to reach out and touch God, or move toward something else that is out there that we desire. But if we simply quiet ourselves, and allow God to touch us and our relationship, we can both grow with each other as we journey down the stream of life, back to God. In doing this, we each open our hearts, and allow ourselves to be loved by each other and by God.

Part of the stereotyping of male and female is that men have to work more than women on sharing their feelings and showing understanding and sympathy. We should work at sharing with our partners our fears, our hurts, and any confusions we may have. Often men have a more difficult time letting go of the need to always be the best, working to achieve the highest level. The couples, especially the Blacks and the Golds, whom I saw found that they needed to let go of these things more and more as they went along in life.

Sometimes life is like a ladder against a tall wall. The higher I get on the ladder, the more I achieve as a male. But I sometimes wonder whether the ladder is on the right wall, or if I want to continue the whole process! This doesn't mean that I want to quit what I am doing in my stage of life—it simply means that I am beginning to realize that there may be another pattern. Instead of using what I would call "Jacob's Ladder," I might use another pattern, which might be called "Sarah's Dancing Circle." Everybody is in a circle dancing, and I may invite you in. If we are a couple, and we are in a circle dancing, we might invite others into the circle—which we can't do if we are competing on a ladder. We are able to invite our extended families into the circle—not his family or her family, but our family. Or, it might be friends, or children, whomever we choose to invite into the circle. The circle is not like the ladder, where the higher we get, the more we have to hold on.

In the sexual relationship, we might think that one has to be strong and the other weaker. But we might want to think again about this pattern. Some of us have a high sex drive, and some of us have a low sex drive. Instead of thinking of ourselves as being on the opposite ends of a teeter-totter, we might think about changing our roles. One may be strong and the other weak, and one may be angry and the other loving, but bliss is somewhere in the middle. Suppose we plan to take a young child on a picnic on a Saturday. We mention it to the child on Tuesday that on Saturday, we are taking him or her on a picnic. All week long we think about going to the park, and the child also has the expectation that we are going to go to the park, and have a nice time. Then on Saturday, we go to the park, walk up the hill, cook our lunch outside, and have a wonderful time. After awhile, we walk down the hill, holding hands with the child, and everything seems wonderful.

Sexuality in marriage follows the same pattern. The first thing is the expectation. The expectation can be very short or it can be a little longer, depending on whether there is a high or a low sex drive. The male or the female can have a high sex drive, and it doesn't make any difference. We will experience a plateau, a period of time that can be very pleasurable, where we enjoy each other's bodies. Males tend to be fast during this time—they are often very focused on intercourse, and they want to have it over with quickly. Then they might say, "that was great," roll over, and go to sleep. Females tend to be much slower. The climax is when we actually have the picnic, and males tend to be excited seven to nine seconds, while the female tends to be much slower, fifteen to twenty minutes. But this doesn't have to be a problem—we can learn to appreciate each other's bodies and slow the process down. These male/female differences, and differences in sex drive don't have to get in the way of our pleasure.

The resolution is when we walk away from the picnic,

holding hands. This is a very important step. At first, intercourse is all firecrackers and rockets shooting off. Both male and female can use intercourse just as a tension release. But women more often complain that men roll over afterwards and go to sleep, or leave the room and switch on a Western on the TV. But to the woman, the time afterwards can be the most important part. I believe that aging can actually help couples, because we can learn to appreciate the time afterwards—the male slows down a little bit—he doesn't get overly excited, have sex, and then call it quits. If we practice, we can learn to adjust to each other and enjoy each other. Wholeness takes time; growth takes time.

Virginia Clemente uses the example of a lobster in a paper bag. That is, when we want to have lobster, we go to the store, spend a lot of time looking at the different lobsters, pick one out, take it home, cook it just right, and eat it. We probably put the shells back in the bag, throw them away, and never think about lobster again until the next time we want to have it. Some couples treat sex the same way in their relationship. But the sexual part of our relationship is integrated throughout every aspect of our lives. It involves our values, our speaking, our mental life, our feelings and emotions, our social life, and our physical being. So the whole of us is involved in our sexuality. Intercourse is just the body parts making contact at a particular moment.

Our sexuality is interrelated with the life-cycle stage we are progressing through, from early adulthood into adulthood (which happens psychologically around the age of 29), into late adulthood. As adults, we make commitments to each other, which means we have made a choice and a promise to each other, in complete freedom. But the difficulty most people have in terms of their commitment to each other has to do with the need for the sexual pattern to grow, just like any other part of the relationship. Just like we need to learn to talk together, we need to learn how to be sexual with each other—learning to be careful with each other, to plan, to explore in ways that are comfortable for both. In so doing, the sexual relationship—and the whole relationship—becomes better. There is a certain amount of risk involved, as there is in trying out any new behavior—but we can make this positive by being very careful, gentle, and considerate as we explore each other.

One of the things which is most useful for couples, both young and old, is to massage each other's bodies, in a very slow and gentle way. I believe that it is best at first for us to massage each other without attention to the sexual organs, so that we become comfortable with our own bodies and our partner's body in terms of touch. Much abuse has been done in the area of touch, but we can prevent this by integrating our sexuality with our spirituality, into a wholeness pattern. We might wonder at times whether we made the right choice, but everybody asks that question now and then. Just because we sometimes question our commitment doesn't mean that we have to run away from that choice. We can stay with it, and see where it is going. As we float along the river of life, we are bound to hit some rapids at times, but if we stay with the rapids even though it is scary in the water, we will find that these rapids are usually a growth pattern.

In the usual sense, the words "sexuality" and "sex," refer to genital activity, ending in an orgasm. But sexuality is much more than this. It is the understanding of ourselves in the world as males or females. It is our attitudes about masculinity and femininity—about our own body, and the body of our partner. It is important for our growth that we don't idealize sexuality—we should be realistic and forgiving, realizing that we all make mistakes. The difficulty in talking about intimacy in terms of spirituality and sexuality is that we have not developed a language to discuss this, so that most couples do not learn how to talk to each other about it.

Speaking of spirituality and sexuality, here is a story which married people can use—we might want to follow the example of the camel drivers in this story. There was a group of Englishmen with their camel drivers who were going across the desert. Each day they would get up before sunrise, and the camel drivers would have to get the food ready, feed the Englishmen, take down the tents, and put everything on the camels. After the day's journey, which went on late into the night, the camel drivers would have to unpack the camels, put up the tent, and cook all the food. They did this each day of the week. On Sunday morning, the Englishmen came to the camel drivers, and found them lying in their beds, not getting ready. The Englishmen tried to rush them, saying that they had to get going, because it was almost sunrise. The camel drivers replied, "Today we aren't going to go, because each of the previous days we've rushed and rushed. Today we are going to sit and wait for our souls to catch up with our bodies."

Wholeness

§

Thus far, I have been talking about our journey down the river of life, with a particular partner whom we have chosen, floating next to us. Carl Jung described four stages that each person in the stream of life passes through toward wholeness. The first stage is when we need to face up to who we have been, who we are, and who we can become. The most realistic way to do this is with a partner, because it keeps us extremely honest, and also builds trust in someone else and in ourselves, by building caring. The second stage is a need for involvement and a willingness to be vulnerable. That is, we need to learn to allow ourselves to be loved and cared for, and to love and care for our partner. When we allow our partner to love us and we love our partner in return, it can take us to a higher level. In the third stage, which Jung called working toward our full capacity, we learn to become the best of what we can be. Marriage can bring out our best, because humor, spirituality, and caring can be worked out with a partner in a pleasant way.

"Journaling"—writing about what is going on in our lives —can help us to find hidden treasures that we have carried around that we weren't aware of. As I said in the beginning of the book, each of us has an outer and an inner part. When we write in a journal, the two parts are put together. A journal can be a special, private thing that we don't have to share with anybody unless we want to. Our partners should definitely respect our journal as private.

The fourth stage is what Carl Jung calls grace. Grace is something that we don't have to earn—it is given to us, if we are open to this special help that comes from God, or our own special higher force. One of the nicest things about grace is that it is given to us again and again, especially in relationships. There are special moments that we can experience, when we just know that something is given to us, and that it is very, very special.

In going through this journey of life, we have to learn to love ourselves. This is so important that God made it a commandment. After we learn to love ourselves, we can learn to love the people around us—our spouse and family. And last of all, we learn to love God. I just reversed the commandments of loving God, and our neighbors as ourselves. But I think that we need to begin our work on the human level, so that we can activate the divine, Godly, or grace levels. We have to love ourselves, our neighbors, and our spouses, and we have to love God, but I would also add that we have to love the world around us. It is very important that we be gentle with the environment, because these are the conditions that we work under. Unless we stay in touch with the world around us, and treat it gently, there is a danger that we might bring about too much wear and tear on it—and on ourselves, our partner, even on God.

In creating wholeness for ourselves, we have to deal with the here and now. As we're floating along in our boats, we have to deal with the splashes of water that are coming in, the leaks in our boats, the little things that irritate us—too much sun, too much wind, too much closeness, too much distance. How we deal with what is going on in the present moment is what gives us our spirituality, and our wholeness.

A Story

ॐ

In this chapter, I want to tell a true story. Moses was on top of the mountain talking to the Lord, and the Lord was giving Moses the commandments. He gave Moses four stone plaques, on which were written the twenty Commandments. Now, Moses was trying to carry these plaques down the mountain, two under each arm, but they were heavy and cumbersome to carry. Meanwhile, the people down below were shouting, "Moses, come down here with those commandments!" Moses tried to rush down the mountain with the plaques, and in the process, he ran around a corner into some sand, and lost one of the plaques. It flew into the mountain and broke—so five of the Commandments lay in pieces on the ground. Moses could not carry the remaining plaques and all the pieces of the fourth, so he left the pieces there, and tried to carry the other three plaques down the mountain. As he proceeded, he could hear the people calling more urgently, "Moses, get here with those commandments!" He ran faster, and some sand got into one of his sandals. He skidded and caught the edge of a cactus, and lost control of another plaque—it slid away from him, hit a rock and broke into pieces. Meanwhile, the people chanted even more urgently, "Moses, Moses, get here with those commandments!" In a panic, Moses dashed on with the remaining two plaques, and finally arrived at the bottom of the mountain. He gave the people the ten commandments.

Meanwhile, up on the mountainside, there lay the pieces of the other commandments—numbers eleven to twenty. At one stage, the people got into trouble with God, and he sent them to different parts of the world. Some went here, and others went there. Eventually, we people living out here in the west, especially in Kansas, started wondering if some of these people were sent to Kansas. We were also curious about what happened to those commandments from eleven to twenty. We've come up with a few of the broken pieces which apparently some of the people brought along on their travels all over the world. We've put these pieces together, and we now have the eleventh commandment. We want to pass that on to you, because, after all, Moses had twenty commandments in the story to start with.

The eleventh commandment says that married people are supposed to be very gentle with each other. We should make this one of the commandments now, that we need to practice with our spouses—to be very gentle with ourselves and with our spouse. Because, after all, if it is a commandment, it is true!

We also have the twelfth Commandment. It, too, was all in little pieces—all that we can figure out is that it says that if you run around all day with a loose rock in your shoe, you have a loose rock in your head.

We haven't gotten too far with the other commandments, but we are still looking for pieces. So perhaps we could all look in our own areas to see if we can come up with some of the other ones. We do think that we might have one of the other commandments, which I will talk to you about later on.

So what is the technique we should use so that we can learn to be gentle with ourselves and our partner? I teach all couples who come into my office how to take "ten minute vacations." These are times that we set aside, to quiet ourselves, to go outside and sit on the front steps with our partner, to calm ourselves down. We simply sit there and do nothing. At this time, we don't want to think about the different things we have to do, or errands we have to run, or problems we have with our partner. We will simply sit there together, and watch a bird in a tree. In my office, I can sit in a chair and look across the street, where a number of birds are constantly playing in a tree. I just sit and watch the birds for ten minutes. Putting some quietness in our system does something to help our relationships.

What we bring to our relationship is ourselves. If our own systems are noisy inside, and we are like rattling barrels, that is what we bring to our marriage system. But if we take ten minutes here and there to quiet ourselves, eventually we will be able to take a half a day, or a full day. Many people plan future vacations, and they anticipate having a marvelous time. But they don't practice slowing themselves down in the meantime—and often they are disappointed in their vacations, because they didn't have a very good time. We have to practice to be good at anything. If we want to learn to play basketball or tennis, we have to practice, and we get better as we practice. It is the same process with learning to quiet ourselves. When we practice being quiet, and slowing ourselves down, it helps to calm our minds, and our relationships benefit from that.

Movies and television give us the impression that marriage is simply a matter of finding the right person by chance, and "falling in love." This is not true. Marriage is more of a matter of matching firm values, or having particular goals in common. At first, these goals can be pretty general, but over time they become more specific. The day-to-day way we work toward these goals becomes more and more important as time goes on. Emotions tell us a great deal of what is going on in a relationship, but we decide on a thinking basis that we are committed to each other. Most marital difficulties come from the irresponsibility, irrationality, or immaturity of one spouse or another. One spouse looks at the other and says, "It's your fault," instead of owning up to his or her own role in a problem. For a marriage to grow, we must grow personally—and it is our responsibility to grow, and our partner's responsibility to handle his or her own growth.

In using the commandments I've discussed, one of the major points to remember is to be gentle. When we are gentle with ourselves, we are more comfortable with ourselves, and we tend to handle ourselves better in our relationship. The idea of gentleness extends not only to our spouse and our children, but also to our relatives. We often will think, "There is my family, and then there is my spouse's family." No, these are all relatives of ours! If we use gentleness, we will often receive some of that gentleness back in our relationships with our relatives.

Marriage takes a certain amount of maturity. It takes attention to individual goals, the couple's goals, and long range goals. This is something that needs to be worked at very slowly —in fact, it takes a lifetime. So we should be gentle with ourselves.

I teach couples and individuals who are bothered by things in life a simple exercise. I would ask you to sit on a chair with your feet flat on the floor, and your arms in your lap, nothing crossed. Then, I would slowly teach you to breathe very deeply —to take a deep breath through the nose, hold it a little bit, and exhale through the mouth. This is done three or four times, and each time the breathing is slowed down. When you blow out your breath, all the stress goes out with it. Now, before I start this exercise, I would give you a small, smooth pebble, which you would hold in your hands. As you relax more, I would ask you to close your eyes. About thirty percent of our energy probably flows out of our eyes, so when we cut that out, we can push out all the tension through our breathing. I then would ask you to imagine placing the rock in a special place. For some people, this special and safe place would be a beach; for others, a field, near a brook, or in the woods—a quiet, special place that would be nice to visit, a place to enjoy. As you continue breathing, you would place the rock in the special place, and then crawl up on the rock and sit there. As you sit there quietly, you would observe nature, and listen to the sounds. Sometimes in your imagination, you can hear birds, or the rustle of leaves, or a breeze—you might even feel a breeze on your shoulders. You might feel warm sunlight shining on your arms or your face. You feel the warmth from the rock, and you feel how good it is to be in this place, and you feel comfortable with yourself.

This relaxation process, as you quiet your body down, and as you slow your breathing down and get more comfortable with yourself, is adding gentleness to your nature. After a period of time, you will slowly come back, open your eyes, and start moving your hands and feet—it's important not to get up too quickly at this time, because the circulation is slowed down. Gentleness and quietness is introduced to the system for a period of time.

We can expand this exercise by introducing another person as you are sitting on the rock in your imagination. It could be Jesus, and he might sit down next to you on the rock. The two of you just smile at each other, and say nothing. You tell him nothing about your problems. He just accepts you, and you sit there and experience each other together. After a period of time, Jesus walks out of your imagination, and you slowly bring yourself back to normal consciousness.

This is similar to a self-hypnosis exercise. Nothing harmful can happen because of it, and if it is frightening at any time, we can slowly open our eyes and return to everyday awareness. It is a gentle way to put calmness and gentleness into our systems. Gerald Heard once wrote, ". . . that the light shines through those who have so let themselves be open." In doing the exercise, I will play calm and restful music in the background—music without words. I particularly like a tape by Steven Hal-

91

pern, called "Dawn." It is a relaxing type of music which slowly wanders on and on, and it helps to create that mystic feeling.

A true turning inward is not for self-centered reasons, or for egoism, but to become other-oriented. To do this, we must come into contact with ourselves—our whole body, our heads, hearts, and guts. Carl Jung uses the term "individuation" to describe the process of establishing contact with the whole self.

Judith Lechman, in her book, *The Spirituality of Gentleness,* says, "In the physical world, a delicate balance must be maintained for continued growth. In our spiritual life, we must establish a similar balance between passivity and activeness, so that we may continue to learn of God without pride." In establishing this gentleness, we develop what I call the solitude of heart. This does not depend upon physical isolation, but on our ability to establish a condition whereby we can sit down and quiet ourselves.

Another book that addresses these kinds of techniques is Morton Kelsey's *The Other Side of Silence.* It is a contemporary guide to the different forms of quieting oneself, some of which are called meditations. They are all simply methods to teach ourselves gentleness. But, a word of warning! We cannot force our encounter with ourselves or with God. We have to let go, and let God do it for us.

As we become more comfortable with this gentleness, we are able to drop the mask that we wear (the "persona," in Jung's terms), which we needed before when we didn't know who we were, when we needed to defend ourselves against intimacy. Dropping our mask makes us more vulnerable to ourselves, and open to our partner. As we practice gentleness, we develop what is called an inward principle. There is a paradox here. As we learn to live this principle, we tend to lose our separateness from others. When I explained synchronicity before, I stated that rather than being dependent or independent, we become interdependent. By practicing gentleness, we find ourselves searching for the good within our partners, friends, relatives, and neighbors, and we are less concerned with their faults.

This is a non-judgmental form of Christian community. Gentleness encourages us to become less selfish as we float along the stream of life, to become more considerate of ourselves and others, and finally to express love.

We might use the analogy that we resemble a tree. As the breezes blow in the autumn, our leaves are slowly stripped away, and as we gather up the leaves we slowly start recognizing who we are, and we open ourselves more and more to what is going on in our lives. Then we can turn to our partner and to God with love and openness. This process takes time and there are definite ways that we can cultivate our gentleness. Since it is stated in the commandment to be gentle, it is our obligation to be so—and I think that these are good methods to follow.

The Stream Ahead

≈

I was standing a short distance away from our air-conditioned bus by the pyramids in Egypt, looking out at a desert area. I was wondering how anyone could possibly maneuver through that area. Suddenly, a short distance away, a Bedouin on a camel seemed to appear out of nowhere, weaving his way through some of the sand hills and dunes. He seemed to be heading someplace. I watched him disappear in a different direction, into the sand hills. I could see no path where he had come from, or to where he was going. Later, I asked the bus driver about where this fellow was going. I said I didn't see a road or path. His reply was, "Oh, but he can see the path!"

Just as I was poorly informed about the ways of the desert, so we can be poorly informed about the ways of marriage. It is important that we listen to the stories of other people who have been married a longer or a shorter time than us, and learn from their experiences. Just as we learn from books, articles, and experts, we can learn from other people, but we should just listen to the information. We can process it and use the information to clarify our options, but in the end only the two partners can make decisions about the relationship.

I suggest that we follow our hearts in making many of these decisions. I have been using the example of floating down the stream of life, with our partner floating next to us. My experience in working with couples suggests that often the stream is too fast, and there isn't time to sit down and relax. But it's good to take some time, to get off of the main stream and go into a smaller stream nearby—one that wanders slowly through the countryside, so we can slow down together. This would give us more time to start listening to ourselves and to each other.

During each day, many experiences happen to each of us, and we are often so busy that we don't have time to process these experiences in our hearts. In counseling, I like to tell people to sit back and just process with their hearts what went on, and sometimes, to share this with their partners. This is like floating our two boats off into a side stream, and sharing some stories and experiences that happened to each of us. This sharing is a very deep form of intimacy. I call this reflective listening. It is simply processing with the heart, either by ourselves or with our partner. When we do this, we don't try to change the other's experience, just listen to it. We then learn more about our partner and we both grow in the process. Sometimes we might even have to stop our boat along the shore in this unknown stream, and ask somebody around us for directions. This would be all right!

Life tends to encourage us to stay in the fast stream, and keep moving forward. The fast stream could mean that we are always running somewhere, and doing something. We don't even give ourselves time to sit down and take a deep breath. Reflective listening helps us to take this time, and when we do it with a partner, it can become a very beautiful and loving experience, leading us toward wholeness.

So, as we are floating along this slow stream, we might reach out and pick a flower; we notice the exquisite beauty of this flower, and the innate goodness of it simply because it is a flower. The same thing can happen to us as marriage partners.

Along with the beauty that is in each of us that we share

with our partner, we can learn to share our vulnerabilities, and our hurts when our dreams are shattered, when our projects don't go as we wanted them to. This sharing of our losses, and even our fears, is not done so we can belittle each other, but so that we can learn to accept ourselves and know ourselves better. Just taking this time out on some side stream, and slowing down a little bit, will help us with our self-acceptance. When we work on our self-acceptance, it helps us to accept our partner, both the good qualities and the bad qualities. We might meander a little bit in this process, but it will be worthwhile if we learn to be a bit more accepting of ourselves and our relationship. This meandering on side streams helps us grow—and growth that starts in the heart is part of our spirituality, and helps us move toward wholeness.

Returning Home

ॐ

Just as the stream approaches the ocean, it tends to spread out and flow more slowly. There are many twists and turns; sometimes the stream is long and sometimes it is muddy, but it always enters the ocean. It is the same for us; we all tend to float back in the stream of life, back to God. It is the same as when we return home at the end of the day. Many times one of us returns at one hour, and another at a different hour, but everybody does return home. So, we go back to God in our marriage the same way.

As in any journey, we can have fears and doubts about the journey and even about the direction. We often have fears of the unknown, and just as with children, most fears are easier to deal with if we talk to each other, if we hold hands. In the same way, as we go through our journey of life back to God, that is, when we pass over, if God holds our hand, it is going to be much easier! So, when each of us goes back separately, we will have a reunion, a grand final moment when we throw the total family party, and we are all together again in God's presence.

Just think of the joy that we have when we sit down around a table and watch a small child celebrate his or her birthday, and the joy and happiness of that small child. We in marriage can share that happiness, when we sit around the table with Jesus, and reunite in our love, in a final birthday celebration for all the things to come. Rather than coming home being an ending, it would be a beginning for us. Yes, it will be new, it will be different, and it could be just as beautiful as the feelings we had when we first started our marriage.

When we first get married, we set up our first home, and there is excitement about picking out furniture, colors, getting special decorations—and we start very slowly. So, in the same way, we will have to learn slowly, because it is a new step, the step of decorating our house with God. Rather than looking at Jesus as a bad parent, we can accept him as a good parent. His love is always there for us, from the beginning to the end. If we open the door, it will always be there. The same way, that love will be there for our partner.

I am reminded of a story of a small boy who was standing on a street corner. An older person came up to the street corner. The boy had always been taught to be kind to older people, so he asked, "Can I help you across the street?" The older person looked at him and smiled, and said, "No, thank you, but it was nice of you to ask." The small boy then replied, "Well, in that case, would you mind helping me across the street?"

Just as we are good parents when we help our children across the street, or through the difficulties of life, we have to allow Jesus into our lives, so that he can show us those same good parental qualities of acceptance, kindness, listening, patience, compassion, and respect for each of us as individuals, and the same for our partner. So, when we are all together in that final family reunion, everything will be O.K.! And each of us should remember not to underestimate the uniqueness of the gift and the story of our particular journey that we will bring to this party.

The Fantasy

Imagine sitting in a comfortable place—a chair at home, lying on the davenport—a quiet, relaxing place. In your imagination, somebody has given you a beautiful cabin in the valley. You are wandering up the trail toward the cabin, and as you walk along, you hear birds singing and the trees rustling. As you look around, you see many wild flowers—for instance, wine cups, a certain type of purple, beautiful wild flower. Everything seems to be so perfect, and as you continue walking, you see different animals gazing at you. They aren't really fearful, because there is nothing to fear in this beautiful valley. As you walk farther, you see the cabin, and you notice how perfectly it is nestled in the end of the valley. Everything seems to fit—the color and style of the cabin, and the way it is designed.

As you get closer, you see a beautiful old well in front of the cabin. It has a cover on it, a handle with a rope, and a bucket that goes down into the well. As you get closer, you also notice that the bucket is an authentic, old-fashioned oak bucket. Since it has not been used for a long time, there are openings or spaces between some of the laths on the bucket. But the rope seems to be strong, and it is fastened OK. The handle seems to be in good working order, and as you look down the well, you can feel the coolness of the water coming up from it. You don't know much about wells, but you decide that it would be fun to crank the bucket down into the water. It is always refreshing to have a nice drink of water, especially since you've walked for awhile. So you crank the handle, and the rope slowly plays its way out. There are squeaks as you lower the bucket, and you think that it sounds very rustic, even romantic. You remember that if you let an old bucket soak for awhile, it will start holding water again. So you let it stay down there for awhile, as you wander around the outside of the house for about a half an hour. Later, you begin cranking the bucket up, and you notice that the bucket seems a little heavier this time. When you get it up, you see that the bucket is about half full of water. Soaking it helped it to form the bucket shape again, but the top part leaked out some water. You had packed a tin cup in your backpack, and so you reach in and take a cup full of the nice, clean water. You smell it—it seems to be all right—and you taste it, and oh! it is the most delicious cup of water you've ever tasted. You slowly savor each swallow, and it is so refreshing—you feel as if it's picked up your whole body, your mind, even your soul. You wonder, oh, where has this water been?

Psychologically speaking, the bucket can be thought of as our capacity for imagery—our ability to go down into the subconscious mind and pull up some information. The rope is the link that we use to make contact with our inner depths. The handle is the specific technique that we use to do this. We crank that handle to set the whole process in motion. We might have used meditation or a ten-minute vacation, one of the ways to quiet ourselves, as we discussed earlier. Any well has small rivulets that drain into it and keep it replenished, but eventually some of these will close up if the well is not used. But if we use the well to pull water, these rivulets will open up more and more, and the well will become fully functioning. This describes the way in which we can make full contact with the unconscious in an open fashion. It is my belief that we need to make contact with the unconscious, which is a source of inner strength. As we do that, we need to be very loving and careful with ourselves. With practice it is easier to make this contact, and we feel more and more refreshed as we drink from the well.

In a marriage, first of all, we have to take care of ourselves. We need to decide to sit down, be quiet, and get in contact with those little rivulets—we need that drink of cold, fresh water. While we are doing this, hopefully our partner is doing the same thing. Then we can share a cold, refreshing cup of water. We can be refreshed by the same well or by each other's well.

We need to be in contact not only with ourselves and our partners, but with God (our Higher Power). We do this by quieting ourselves, by sitting down and listening. The commandments say to love God, and our neighbor as ourself. I am saying that we should begin by loving ourselves, then loving our partner, then using our partner to go to God, whom we also love. Each of us is required to manage our own boat as we float down the stream of life. As we are floating, we make contact with a very special person, and this relationship grows over a period of time; it continues on into the afterlife. Each of us decides what we want to do with this special relationship. If we take care of ourselves, we can have a lot of fun along the way. Each of us is in our own boat, but we can splash, we can laugh, I suppose we can fight, we can care for each other, we can talk to each other, we can touch each other.

Intimacy is simply caring for each other, reaching out, expanding our boundaries, and including each other as we float down the river of life; eventually, we float off together into the great beyond.

I have shared with you some of what I have experienced in my work with couples over the past thirty-six years; it is my hope that this will help you find some gentle places along the stream of life. At times, we might get caught by a branch that is hanging out over the river. Other times we might run up against a rock, or we might need to sit out on a rock and rest awhile. Sometimes we might hit the rapids—a crisis. I believe that if we hang on through the rapids, we will always find calmer water, especially if we work on our own personal growth. This work is not selfishness—it is self-affirmation.

The river always continues—it the same way with the marriage. If we go gently, God is always there to help us. There is always a third hand reaching out to us—there are other people who care very deeply about us. Our vocation in marriage is God's dream for us—and each of us is very, very special in the dream of God. God has the imagination to come up with a plan for each of us, but you and your partner carry out the reality of what is. So, enjoy it!

A Marriage Vocation

୫~

Definition: A vocation takes a lifetime;
   —not a "once-and-for-all" call
   —a lifelong conversation
   In early adulthood, we imagine what we would like in a marriage. In middle adulthood, we reimagine what we want in a marriage. In late adulthood, we affirm in retrospect.

—Sean Sammon, Ph.D.

Suggestions for Further Readings

⚜

Thomas Berry, *Befriending the Earth* (Twenty-Third, 1991).

Robert Bly, *Iron John* (Addison-Wesley, 1990).

Henry James Borys, *The Way of Marriage* (Purna, 1991).

Susan Campbell, *The Couples' Journey* (Impact, 1980).

Irene Claremont de Castillejo, *Knowing Woman* (Harper & Row, 1973).

Carol Gilligan, *In a Different Voice* (Harvard University Press, 1982).

James Greteman and Joseph Dunne, *When Divorce Happens* (Ave Maria, 1990).

James Greteman and Leon Haverkamp, *Divorce and Beyond* (ACTA, 1983).

William Houff, *Infinity in Your Hand* (Melior, 1989).

Morton Kelsey, *Reaching* (Harper & Row, 1983).

Morton Kelsey, *The Other Side of Silence* (Paulist, 1985).

Judith Lechman, *The Spirituality of Gentleness* (Harper & Row, 1987).

Harriet Lerner, *The Dance of Anger* (Perennial, 1986).

Harriet Lerner, *The Dance of Intimacy* (Harper, 1989).

Frank Main, *Perfect Parenting & Other Myths* (Comp Care, 1986).

James B. Nelson, *The Intimate Connection* (Westminster, 1988).

Anthony Padovano, *Love and Destiny* (Paulist, 1987).

M. Scott Peck, *The Road Less Traveled* (Simon & Schuster, 1978).

John Powell, *Happiness Is An Inside Job* (Tabor, 1989).

John Powell, *The Secret of Staying in Love* (Argus, 1974).

Paula Ripple, *Growing Strong at Broken Places* (Ave Maria, 1989).

John Sanford, *The Invisible Partners* (Paulist, 1980).

John Sanford and George Lough, *What Men Are Like* (Paulist, 1988).

Anne Wilson Schaef, *Escape from Intimacy* (Harper & Row, 1989).

Deborah Tannen, *You Just Don't Understand* (Ballantine, 1990).